Eric Owen Moss

Paola Giaconia

Eric Owen Moss
The Uncertainty of Doing

Cover
The Box, 1990-1994
Culver City, California

Flap
Samitaur Complex: Phase I, 1989-1996
Los Angeles, California

Back flap
Queen's Museum of Art, Contest project
(detail), 2003-
Queens, New York

Editor
Luca Molinari

Design
Marcello Francone

Editing
Marta Cattaneo

Layout
Paola Ranzini

Translations
Lucian Comoy
for Language Consulting, Milan

To Miller, the Bonono Man

I wish to thank my parents,
Donatella and Saverio, for having
given me the possibility of studying
in Los Angeles, where I trained
as architect; Marco, for having
put up with me during the months
of intense work dedicated to this
book; Lorenzo Spagnoli, for all
his useful advice; Luca Molinari,
for the confidence he showed
in my project; Dolan Daggett, Eric
McNevin and Leif Halverson from
the Eric Owen Moss Architects
studio for the kindness, precision
and rapidity with which they
always answered my question

First published in Italy in 2006 by
Skira Editore S.p.A.
Palazzo Casati Stampa
via Torino 61 – 20123 Milano, Italy
www.skira.net

Printed and bound in Italy. First edition

ISBN-13 978-88-7624-276-2
ISBN-10 88-7624-276-7

Distributed in North America by Rizzoli
International Publications, Inc., 300 Park
Avenue South, New York, NY 10010
Distributed elsewhere in the world by
Thames and Hudson Ltd., 181a High
Holborn, London WC1V 7QX, United
Kingdom

Contents

Introduction

Foreword

"Contemporary architects have often felt obliged to demonstrate a chronology of building logic without acknowledging what underlies that logic. [...] I am looking for an argued chronology in which consistency is variable."[1]

"I don't think my work reflects progress in a teleological sense. It reflects a belief only in internal and individual progress, which is sometimes associated with re-gress, in a real sense and in a psychoanalytic sense. But, sometimes, by going backward, you're going forward. In fact, sometimes the only way to go forward is to go backwar."[2]

Monday 17 January 1994 (Los Angeles, California), 4.30 a.m.
Los Angeles is struck by a tremendous earthquake with its epicenter at Northridge, with shock waves of an intensity of 6.7 on the Richter scale lasting about 40 seconds. Herbert Muschamp, architecture critic for the "New York Times",[3] has an appointment with Eric Owen Moss the following morning to visit some of his latest projects in Culver City, including The Box, which has just been finished. Moss is able to dedicate a few hours of his time to his guest: it is a national holiday—Martin Luther King's Day—and the office is quieter than usual. Eric arrives on time at 9 a.m. and, unlike Muschamp, who is visibly shaken by the strong earthquake which had woken him in the middle of the night, Eric is calm and relaxed. And how could it be otherwise, concludes Muschamp, given that his buildings seem to have survived an earthquake?[4]

Writing a monograph about an architect usually means explaining each stage in his career in a linear method, from the start of his projects to his most recent work. In an attempt to illustrate the evolution of his work, the analysis seeks almost always to establish some relationships between the salient moments of the architect's professional life in order to offer a reading of a systematic and coherent relationship between the works, and a map of his professional development so as to be able to project his future evolution.

The case of Eric Owen Moss is very different. It is impossible, by examining his work chronologically, to find an evolutionary logic to it. And it would be extremely hard, as well as useless, to adopt this procedure to discuss his work. Moss proposes an architecture that is free of consolidated points of reference and featuring strong elements of indeterminateness, ambiguity and apparent casualness.

The figure of Moss, set against the contemporary architectural panorama, is interesting for the up-to-date nature of his thinking, which sees the need to adapt with imagination to constantly changing conditions; and these conditions, because of their mutability, oblige the architect to offer solutions that can only ever be temporary, never definitive.

It is inevitable that architecture today should move within a constant shifting of events: its field of application is always uncertain, without order and in constant transformation. The feature that makes Moss's work stand out is the boldness with which his design hypotheses allow for contingencies and leave space for the occurrence of a new, provisional order, without hindering it. Moss works almost like a tightrope walker, continuing to experiment as if pushed by a profound desire to constantly test himself. His projects recodify architectural research within a tremendously unstable contemporaneity and his production over the years takes on a development whose strongly disjointed logic is hard to perceive. Every work, indeed, seems to spring from a curious and unrepeatable concatenation of circumstances and the arbitrariness, although only apparent, seems programmatically predisposed to overthrow all rules.

This book, therefore, does not seek to give an interpretation of Eric Owen Moss's architecture, setting his production within a historical perspective with a linear development. Rather, the aim is to discover the theoretical and architectural problems within his production and activity to which he has given form, at the same time as defining his poetic intentions and unusual procedural approach that is so deeply rooted in the personality of the singular figure of Eric Owen Moss.

Phobos and L.A. School

"I am intent on constructing the conflict between object and pre/post object, between what is recognizable as an existing type, known to history, and a pre/post historic postulate which suggests that the form itself is not static. History is in motion, so space is in motion. My aim is to build that motion in architecture."[5]

"Architecture can deliver the mix—a need to comprehend, and the inability to comprehend. That's architecture's job at the end of the twentieth century."[6]

Friday 29 August 1997 (Culver City, California), 3 p.m.
It is a hot day in Los Angeles. This is the one week during the year in which the unbearable Santa Ana—a hot, dry wind—blows in from the desert east of Los Angeles. I live in a small glazed house in Mar Vista, one of the few designed by Gregory Ain in 1947 to have survived perfectly intact. The shade offered by the majestic eucalyptus trees planted for Garret Eckbo's landscape project in the front yard is of no help. Seeking some way to cool down, I leave my house and go to find a person I recently met in this city which is to be my home for the next three years.
This person is Tom Farrage, a friendly architect of Lebanese origin and a graduate of SCI-Arc. Tom has a studio/workshop at Culver City, in which

Phobos, one of the two satellites of Mars (courtesy: NASA/JPL-Caltech)

the room, with computers, is separated with a glass panel from his carpentry shop where this artist/metal craftsman makes complex structures he has designed himself or for other architects, including Morphosis, Israel and Moss. Tom is very pleased to see me and, with the hospitality and friendliness that distinguish him, offers me a coffee: a real coffee, he stresses, made using his wonderful Cimbali espresso machine with Illy arabica coffee Tom has had sent specially from Italy. Soon, another guest appears at his welcoming kitchen/bar overlooking the road. "He's one of my neighbors", explains Tom, introducing him to me, "a famous architect: Eric Owen Moss". I had recognized him, having frequently seen his photo published in magazines, and now I have the honor to have him sitting next to me. The conversation flows smoothly. Eric is very affable and certainly a great talker. He immediately fascinates me for the passion and enthusiasm with which he describes his work. I cannot turn down his invitation to go with him next door, to 8557 Higuera Street, where he has his office. Studio models (lots of them), sketches pinned to the wall, computers operated by young architects reveal complex volumetric compositions that Moss deforms with an almost virtuoso mastery. I am introduced to the studio's press officer, a polite bespectacled young man Moss asks to accompany me on a tour around Culver City. This is my first pilgrimage to this part of town. I visit various buildings, from the oldest to the most recent: the Samitaur Building, The Box, the Pittard Sullivan building. Not just the exteriors but also the interiors (which I am privileged to be able to visit with a kind, knowledgeable guide) strike me for their apparent rejection of any grammatical logic or rule. It's a fine afternoon (I have almost forgotten the unbearable heat) which ends on the pentagonal terrace of the Samitaur. From here, there is a splendid view of Culver City and one would wish to be able to imagine what forms its future might take on.

There's a picture Eric Moss likes to show and describe at some length in his frequent public presentations and conferences. It is a photograph of Phobos, one of Mars's two satellites.

Phobos[7] is very different than what NASA scientists expected before the two Viking spacecrafts landed on the surface of the red planet in 1976 and transmitted images of its two satellites the following year. Phobos is not spherical but is instead a large jagged mass of irregular form, and its rotation is in the opposite direction. The strongly appealing and poetic image and the deep fascination it exerts on Moss say much about his personality and manner of working.

Similarly to Phobos, Moss's designs bear within them the sign of a solitude. They express a sometimes elusive complexity, emerge from radical tectonic mutations (leading to systematic typological redefinitions) and seem to express a suffocated desperation. But then, like the satellite that fixes relationships with its planet, generated by the laws of astronomical physics, Moss's buildings also seek a dialogue with their context. If we take the case of Culver City, they express a strong urban value. Indeed, they themselves create it.

Like Phobos, which upset all of NASA's scientific forecasts, Moss is an unusual, unconventional architect hard to catalogue within the ambiguous, complex cultural panorama marking the history of architecture in the late 20th century.

Even within the so-called L.A. School, Moss is a singular, rather atypical figure. The term, L.A. School, was coined in the early 1990s to describe the generation of L.A. architects beginning to work after Frank O. Gehry, those who many critics dubbed the Gehry Kids[8]. With the vitality of his early works (starting with the projects for the Danzinger Studio in Hollywood and for his home in Santa Monica, paradigms of a new sensitivity), Gehry overturned the canons of architectural language, marking a fundamental new turning point. He freed the practice of architecture from the rigid dogma regulating the relationship between form, function and materials and supplied a fundamental contribution to the renewal of an "architectural language now approaching exhaustion"[9], marking a break and opening the road to experimentation by other young architects.

Thanks to the impetus provided by the Gehry case, the architectural culture of L.A. developed rapidly, above all through the work of architects such as Morphosis[10], Frank Israel and Eric Owen Moss. Strengthened by a rich and well-rooted building tradition, as well as by a varied environment that was rich in stimuli and suggestions, in the space of just a few years it revealed itself to be "not reducible to one sole, important talent".[11] The buildings of these architects—with their bold spaces, irreverent towards any form of stability, metaphors of the complexity and economic, political and cultural tensions of society—were able to interpret and materialize the profound changes under way in the contemporary city,[12] as well as its precariousness and dissolution. What resulted was a consistent and vigorous architectural production that soon knocked down the wall of silence raised by the presumptuous East Coast, which had always relegated Californian culture in general (and not just architecture) to a position of secondary importance. The establishment of the new-born SCI-Arc school of architecture, founded in 1972[13] by the orthodox modernist, Ray Kappe, and immediately gaining a reputation for its degree courses and anti-academic specialization, contributed to the formation of a new generation of architects who moved through an unexplored territory, far beyond the borders of canonical modernism.

The term school (in L.A. School) suggests, however, that there is a movement of similar style, and that its exponents all share a comparable way of thinking. Upon closer inspection, this term has over time[14] revealed some weak points and is in some ways limiting. The various protagonists, gathered under the umbrella of this definition, dispute the identity of the school and trend—which nevertheless brought them international fame—and have all, as may be seen, followed different avenues, although sharing a new way of tackling "the relationship between type, form and function as mutating entities, subject to the pressures of a dynamic patronage that is undergoing rapid metamorphosis".[15] They are also clearly distinct from the glossy images of post-modernism of the early 1980s. The definition is, however, acceptable in a broader sense, if we consider a shared sensibility—that to the contradictoriness, discontinuity and dispersion of the heterogeneous L.A. context, to mention just one—which has, nevertheless, given rise to a composite linguistic expression and a varied panorama of objectives.

Moss in particular stands apart from the L.A. School for at least two sets of reasons.

In the first place, while the others (Israel, Mayne, Rotondi) were experimenting prevalently with single family homes (the testing ground of the young avant-garde in Los Angeles since the times of Schindler and Neutra), which reveal the marks of an interesting research and experimentation, Moss worked within a precise area—the manufacturing district of Culver City—creating projects that were rich in urban value and marked a process of rebirth and renewal of the metropolitan fabric. Thus, while most of the projects realized by the protagonists of the 1980s were dotted throughout the city, often isolated on the hills of Santa Monica or Hollywood—and may be appreciated as convincing examples of linguistic and typological experimentation—the work of Moss immediately stood out for its urban potential.

Thanks to the visionary patronage of a business couple, Frederick and Laurie Samitaur Smith, Eric Moss was able to design and develop an important project of urban transformation over a number of years, in an area that in the 1980s was the shapeless, chaotic post-industrial territory of Culver City. His bold (like follies insisting on a courageous typological and spatial experimentation) and yet strict incursions (the projects are all part of an ambitious project for the progressive re-conversion of the manufacturing district) gave rise to an interesting urban reform plan conceived as an entity undergoing constant redefinition and modification, an effervescent work in progress of which many of the pieces have been realized.

"This is about grabbing the land and doing something with it, but not in a CIAM kind of way. This is about being ecumenical", says Moss.

Secondly, Moss stands out for his approach to architecture, which is empirical and personal in style, and derives neither from pre-established dogma or criteria, nor from a desire to compare himself with other styles of producing architecture. His oeuvre cannot be easily assimilated to a precise line of research; his work shows, indeed, how the architect's intention is not that of following a single and coherent line of reasoning, and nor that of creating his own formal "style" that may be used anywhere without distinction.

"What I don't want to do is give you back something that is monochromatic, single-minded (somehow single-colored and simple-minded are close to each other) so that if something is simply symmetrical, or simply balanced, or simply linear, or simply a narrative, then it's simple-minded. My experience of the world is not that".[16]

Thus, for example, in a sort of simplified historical genealogy, the Aronoff Guest House may be seen as a baroque and paradoxical interpretation of the visionary architecture of Claude Nicolas Ledoux, although it does not share the same predilection for simple, pure, ideal geometric forms. Indeed, while with the project for the Maison des gardes agricoles[17] in the

Conjunctive Points, Culver
City, California

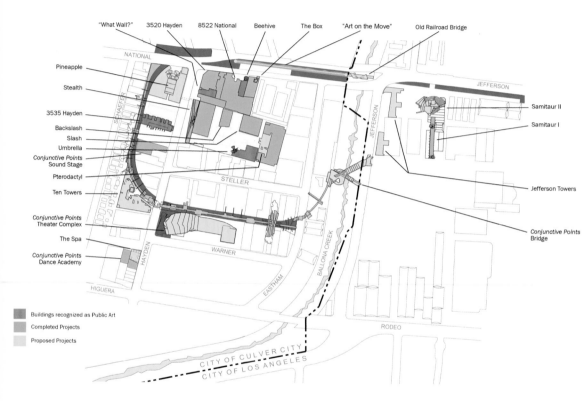

"What Wall?"   3520 Hayden   8522 National   Beehive   The Box   "Art on the Move"   Old Railroad Bridge

Pineapple

Stealth

3535 Hayden

Backslash

Slash

Umbrella

Conjunctive Points
Sound Stage

Pterodactyl

Ten Towers

Conjunctive Points
Theater Complex

The Spa

Conjunctive Points
Dance Academy

NATIONAL

SCHAEFER

STELLER

HAYDEN

WARNER

HIGUERA

EASTHAM

BALLONA CREEK

JEFFERSON

JEFFERSON

RODEO

Samitaur II

Samitaur I

Jefferson Towers

Conjunctive Points
Bridge

CITY OF CULVER CITY
CITY OF LOS ANGELES

Buildings recognized as Public Art

Completed Projects

Proposed Projects

12

ideal village in the Parc de Maupertuis (1780) Ledoux sacrificed any functional aspect in favor of a purely symbolic architecture, the geometric matrix of Moss's Aronoff Guest House is manipulated and denatured to the point that it almost loses its identity, and the sphere placed on the hillside suggests a sense of instability and imbalance. Again, the Ince Theater recalls the Total Theater project designed by Walter Gropius for Erwin Piscator in 1927, with its single, flexible space aiming at the maximum participation of the spectator in the action on stage; the complex articulation of volumes in the Samitaur Building seems a re-interpretation of Borromini's facades; the sloping surfaces of the Stealth a contemporary revisitation of Guarini; and the infrastructure proposed by the S.P.A.R.City project, which winds between the industrial buildings of Culver City like a snake, cannot but recall John Nash's terraces.[18]

The astronomical image of Phobos almost has a value as an epistemological metaphor. Transposed into the world of architecture, it offers a different manner of observing, feeling and understanding a universe in which new probable forms of relationship are slowly establishing themselves, while the traditional equilibria (within the L.A. setting often characterized by a social, natural and geological instability[19]), although precarious, have been lost. Thus, in Culver City, Moss becomes the director of an urban plan which, although benefiting from a global vision, moves forward in little fragments. And with the realization of every successive fragment, the plan is ready to change, taking into consideration the new requirements that have appeared over time, and adjusting to the surrounding conditions that are always changeable and never known beforehand.

"A final conceptual resolution is not available to me. Rather, the architecture moves when the paradigm moves. And the paradigm, however powerful, is provisional. So I keep looking",[20] says Moss.

"But in the case of Moss, the need to distinguish himself from neomodernist architects on the one hand and expressionist deconstructionists on the other has generated a different note, one that perhaps signals a slight shift in the framing of fin-de-siècle apologetics."[21]

22 October 1978 (Los Angeles, California). The architecture critic of "The Los Angeles Times", John Dreyfuss, publishes an article[22] in which he writes of the young Eric Owen Moss. In particular, he describes an "exuberant" building designed by him with the then partner, Jim Stafford, on Main Street in downtown Los Angeles. The project, which has just been awarded a Progressive Architecture Design citation,[23] is described by Dreyfuss as "a dash of exuberance and enthusiasm in an unlikely neighborhood: the monotonous block of Main Street between 11th and 12th Streets that has grown up over the years as expressionless as a clique of dull men. To that humdrum block of flatfaced buildings on the edge of Los Angeles' huge garment district, Moss brought a splash of color, an excitement of design and a touch of mystery that add up to exuberance and enthusiasm".

Eric Owen Moss[24] has been able to build a modus operandi that has not lost sight of its origins over the years, and which has instead become richer over time without forgetting the youthful torments and trepidation from which it has drawn stimuli and impulses.

At the end of the 1960s, in the midst of the student demonstrations, Moss was at Berkeley, one of the most active settings of the revolt in the US. Here, he studied with, amongst others, Paffard Keatinge Clay, pupil of Le Corbusier and collaborator of Wright at Taliesin, who struck the young student for his idealistic vision of architecture. In 1969, the year after Moss earned his Master of Architecture, Clay's expansion project for the San Francisco Art Institute was begun, the outstanding feature of which was the stepped roof of the lecture hall providing an amphitheatre on the outside. In those same years, Clay was commissioned by the San Francisco State University to design the Student Union building, inaugurated in 1975. The project, characterized by the presence of two inclined tetrahedrons pointing towards the sky, struck Moss for its boldness and strong expressive charge, a true exception within the moderate context of San Francisco.

After Berkeley, Moss went to Harvard to attend the Graduate School of Design. And here appears another of the recurrent images in his tales, an image dating from his years as a student at Cambridge, Massachusetts. It is that of the Ise Shrine, a timber framed traditional Japanese temple near Kyoto, Japan. This Taoist shrine, the original construction of which dates back to the 7th century A.D., is demolished and rebuilt on a neighboring patch of land every 20 years. And thus, "the building is fixed, constant, unmoving, and eternal, and at the same time it is in flux, ephemeral, changing, and limited",[25] says Moss.

"The faithful adherence throughout the ages to the custom of rebuilding the Ise Shrine every twenty years is a sign that the Japanese were not interested in preserving old buildings as such. It was the style, not the actual structures embodying it that they sought to preserve for posterity. Everything that had physical, concrete form, they believed, was doomed to decay; only style was indestructible. Fire can destroy a wooden building in a matter of minutes: the philosophy of the impermanence of all things was a solace to a people that built only in wood. A Westerner would probably insist that style is inseparable from physical, concrete form, but, to go one step further, what the Japanese wanted to preserve was not even the style as such in all its details but something else, some intangible essence within its style"[26], declares Kenzo Tange.

The visit to the Ise Shrine, a metaphor of change, was highly stimulating for the intellectual growth of Eric Owen Moss, leading him from a young age to appreciate that sense of precarious equilibrium at the edge between memory of the past and the creative impulse characterizing so much of his current production.

We may take the Pittard Sullivan building in Culver City (1994-1997) as an example, a project in which the new is a hybrid, inevitably distant from the coherence and conventionality of the original structure, yet strongly dependent upon it in an always palpable tension. The four pre-existing buildings on the lot were demolished and the sole elements that survived of the original constructions were a brick wall and the double arched trusses in wood. A new shell was built on this old structure, left as a memory of the manufacturing past of this part of town. The ends of the old wooden beams are allowed to emerge like shreds of the anonymous history of industrial buildings.

Or we can look at the project called What Wall? (1998), again in Culver City, located in a former warehouse. The bulging volume, comprising 1000 concrete blocks measuring 20 cm per side, is a sort of protuberance on the smooth façade facing the street, an unexpected anomaly rendered even more surprising by the maintenance of the generic construction with which it contrasts. It contains the management offices which, thanks to the openings in the undulating wall, enjoy natural lighting.

Or again, the more recent project for the expansion of the 19th-century Patent Office Building at the Smithsonian Institution in Washington D.C. (2003) which, despite the scrupulous compositional precision dictated by the need to respond in a coherent way to the exhibition requirements of the institution, is characterized by a stimulating visual, energetic and strongly expressive impact. The physical nature of the building in which the central courtyard is inserted constitutes the backdrop for the spectacle offered by the calm, aerial and diffuse seduction of the glass roof and of the five new volumes of the gallery suspended on the first floor: beams with structural elements in glass which, in a strongly expressive vision, seem to challenge the laws of statics; secluded, intimate settings offering the public the perception of a continuous space.

Since his earliest works,[27] Moss showed a predilection for a form of architecture characterized by strong, bold gestures, a passion for expressionist and extremely individual forms that do not seek to set up a dialogue with the pre-existing or with the surroundings but which, rather, highlight and make the most of their differences.

"I think that there's a consciousness that whatever you do, you always arrive in the middle. Or if it is not the middle, you always arrive in the midst of a site where there are other buildings, a history where there is a pre-history and a post-history. So you always land into something and begin to have to understand it both in terms of what preceded you and in terms of the opportunity to remake the record."[28]

A Mix of Stimuli

"The artist is always beginning. Any work of art which is not a beginning, an invention, a discovery is of little worth."[29]

"Gnostic architecture is not about faith in a movement, a methodology, a process, a technique, or a technology. It is a strategy for keeping architecture in a perpetual state of motion."[30]

Wednesday 21 January 1998 (Culver City, California), 2 p.m.
Aboard an old blue 1987 Toyota, in the company of Wei-Li Liao and of Toshiko Hidaka, I reached the junction of National and Hayden. Eric Owen Moss made an appointment for us all, students in his architecture studio at SCI-Arc, to meet him in front of a peculiar building on which the builders are still busily working. The work is anything but simple: the position of the almost 1000 blocks of concrete (20 cm per side) forming the soft, deformed building bubble, is described in 52 pages of construction documents to demonstrate the fact—Moss explains to us—that the apparent expressive freedom in architecture requires strict control.
Moss has inserted an extraneous object within the pre-existing ordinary building shell: a new, deformed, strident structure that does not aspire to integrate and resolve itself, but rather alters the former building with vigor and passion. We students immediately understood that our project (for the Jewish Museum of San Francisco, housed within a building that was to be enlarged) would not be a simple affair.

Moss pursues a very personal approach to his work that is completely disassociated with the categorizations that have sought to enclose his production. He is open to varied experiences and heterogeneous references, and works by experimenting with his interests arising from a blend of stimuli coming from a range of fields besides architecture. His sensibility reacts in response to suggestions from music, poetry, art, science and mathematics, and the new epistemological sectors these sciences have traced out. Architecture thus opens itself to new contaminations, generating unexpected results.

Over the years, Moss has produced a consistent critical reflection on architecture that has never concealed his deep interest in modern literature (Samuel Beckett, James Joyce), poetry (Ezra Pound, Thomas Stearns Eliot), music (John Cage), and sculpture (Henry Moore). From this base, he has demonstrated a constant attention in the conceptual and theoretical value of the project as a venue for personal reflection.

What complex process of elaboration makes it possible to transpose musical, literary, artistic and scientific experiences into the architect's work? What theoretical and design reflections have stimulated this plurality of visions? It would be hard to disentangle the dense, complex intertwining of influences and inspirations underlying Eric Owen Moss's architecture. In his work, indeed, there are some constant references, but also a continuous search for something from which to always re-interpret his own thinking.

In recent years, Moss has often mentioned his interest in Henry Moore's *The Helmet*. A helmet is an easily recognizable object and simple in that its form conforms to that which it contains: in substance, the form of the head (content) and of the helmet (container) are congruent. Henry Moore, however, gives a very different interpretation to this simple artifact: the content of the helmet may be perceived through the hole in the external surface, but can never be comprehended in its totality, in part because there are various discontinuous areas between container and content. In practice, the internal form is enveloped in the external one, but the two are different and separate; the inside and the outside are at the same time coincident and discontinuous.

Henry Moore, *The Helmet*

The architect explains his project for the Samitaur Building and its complex volumetric articulation by suggesting an interesting parallel with this work by Moore. The new spatiality offered by the building, indeed, offers many analogies with this three-dimensional work which Moss analyses in an almost scientific manner, dissecting it and revealing the presence of a series of zones: "the outside of the outside, the inside of the outside, the outside of the inside, the inside of the inside". The feature that ties all these elements together is the space under continuous tension that is created between them and which becomes a sort of glue. The Samitaur Building can also be dissected into a series of pieces: the stilts, the stairs, the pool, etc. All these elements do not peacefully co-habit, however. It is the glue, the space in tension that enables them "to cohere and become a building".[31]

And sculpture is useful to Moss also for the re-interpretation of another one of his buildings: The Box. Re-interpretation, because Moss came to know this work by Moore only after he had produced his project in Culver City. Once he discovered and appreciated it in all its geometric and spatial ambiguity, it became—*a posteriori*—a useful reference for the architect.

Eric Moss is also a connoisseur of John Cage, but he looks at the work of this unusual musician with the eyes of the architect: he analyses the score and, observing the graphic signs organizing the notes, draws aesthetic suggestions from them. Indeed, Moss speaks of "visual music". "It's a graphic association of notes connecting points with lines and points with other points visually, so that the visual aesthetic of the music has a substantial role in determining what the auditory aesthetic is. [...] Cage is asking what music is. Is it what is written, what is played, what we hear, what is heard and remembered, or what one sees?"[32].

In his proposal for the World Trade Center, musical notation was re-interpreted by Moss not merely as an auditory experience, but as a visual one too; Cage's scores were read as an elaborate transposition evoking forms and spaces. Moss asked himself what producing a design for the World Trade Center meant. "What is the project? Is there a historical antecedent? Is there an American historical antecedent?"[33]. The trauma following 9/11 struck the American collective psyche hard, causing Americans to lose their certainty of the linearity of history and a faith in the control of their own destiny, and this has induced them to accept a precarious vision of things. It was very hard, therefore, concluded Moss, to produce a plan. The adequate forms are unknown; perhaps they have not yet been invented. Cage's score provided a starting point to conceive a visual, conceptual idea: "there will be music again". The diagrammatic image is strongly appealing. A series of elements may be recognized in it: a plan of a city ("any city, all cities, New York City"), a portion of a frame of curtain wall that survived at ground zero, the score, red coloring (blood?) running and penetrating into the bowels of the earth. But then the suggestion also becomes spatial: Moss's idea was that the site had to become a park and amphitheatre; and temporal: the four shadows (two for each of the towers struck, one shadow marking the time when the tower was hit, and the other marking the time when the tower collapsed) recall the tragic sequence of the events and are what remains of what was. "Make of that what you will", wrote Moss in his statement accompanying the project. And he did so not with the ambiguity or fake modesty frequently adopted by many architects for reasons of vanity. "Make of that what you will" was for Moss a fundamental part of the project, which lives and is built around this opportunity.

Moss's poetics and language also make use of literature, and are significantly enriched by these influences which bring great freedom to the project. In some ways, his means of expression are somehow similar to the complexity of the writings of Joyce.

In the same way as Joyce in Ulysses takes an existing story as his starting point and then intervenes on a given complexity, adopting, interpreting and multiplying it, so Moss works in a similar way in many of his projects in Culver City. For example we may take the Pittard Sullivan building, in which the form resulting from the design process maintains the original imprint: the portions of the former building are a sort of genetic memory of the old structure and make it possible to measure the completed change. Or we may observe the facades of Slash & Backslash, in which a clean slash lays bare the original wooden structure to the exterior, which remains in all its estranged nudity. Or again, the project for the Pterodactyl, in which the base of the building, intended for car parking, offers a simple, repetitive structural grid, with regular bays analogous to those of the surrounding warehouses, suddenly agitated by the geometric and structural complexity of the nine suspended rectangular boxes containing the offices.

Joyce's ability to "dash readers' hopes of signifying linearity, order, syntax and sense"[34] can also be discerned in Moss's work in the Lawson Westen House, where the design is never wholly understandable in its entirety by observing the single parts, each of which seems to almost contradict the other. The curved beam of the ceiling, for instance, comprises three parts, each of which alone is insufficient to explain the entire composition. Moreover, the sketches for The Box reveal a design method that proceeds by realizing a series of unexpected subversions within an initial "figure" that is apparently clear and comprehensible. Something similar occurs in James Joyce when, for example, a strict order (the same as in Homer's epic), becomes the framework on which to attach a series of surprising spatial and temporal upsets.

Le Corbusier's drawing, which placed Dionysus and Apollo in what was for him a preferable bilateral symmetry, was radically altered by Moss. Rationality now sails in an immense Dionysian sea.

Moss abandons the convenience of a sort of deductive process which, without too many surprises and in a linear manner, can lead towards a conventional order of things. This is what he, in what is perhaps a provoca-

Proposal for the World
Trade Center contest

tive manner, describes as the "Penelope theory of architecture": it is a metaphor that compares Odysseus's faithful wife, who at night undid the shroud she wove during the day, to the architect who, when he designs, "makes something and dismantles it simultaneously".[35]

"You are making something and then contesting its validity. This is not like saying I have no sense of where the project is going. It doesn't mean everything's possible. Maybe it means everything's a possible beginning".[36] Despite the strong and sophisticated intellectual charge of his works, it is undeniable that Moss sees architecture not only as a discipline which in substantial measure includes a constructed theory, a conceptual base, but also—and above all—as an eminently empirical activity.

Thanks to his ability to always look at his design tasks with fresh eyes, as well as his conscious acceptance of all the elements of unpredictability and indeterminacy that are part of each project, Moss was in the best of conditions to carry forward a major urban design plan such as that for Culver City.

Dionysius and Apollo

The Great Commisions in Culver City

"What is fortunate about Los Angeles is that it is not a city with a long history, it doesn't obligate architects in the way that almost every other city does. [...] There's not a lot which is obligatory and compelling either in terms of a structure of buildings, a quality of design, a pedigree of exceptional work. [...] In my case [...] it was really very much up to me to make a definition for what constituted the building idea, the city planning idea, organizational strategies, program strategies."[37]

"Los Angeles is not distilled, not fixed, hasn't assigned particular weights. L.A. is a city in motion that makes and remakes itself. L.A. has always had an apprehension for what is fixed and durable as a useful element in the making of a city."[38]

"[...] There is, it seems to us,
At best, only a limited value
In the knowledge derived from experience.
The knowledge imposes a pattern, and falsifies,
For the pattern is new in every moment
And every moment is a new and shocking
Valuation of all we have been [...]"[39]

> Monday 4 May 1987 (Culver City, California), 11 a.m.
> Eric is in his studio, in full creative flood. He is walking between the desks at which his assistants are finishing one of the many study models of the Central Housing Office for the University of California at Irvine. Eric is still not completely satisfied and convinced of some of the design choices. He removes a wall from the model, slices it with a paper knife and studies it in its new composition of solids and voids. He retires to his office to continue to reflect. After a short while, accompanied by a young German trainee, a youthful looking man, tall and powerfully-built, enters. Frederick Samitaur Smith has come for the rent and this time has come in person in order to meet his tenants. He is struck by the drawings on the studio walls. In particular, his eye falls on Eric's desk, on which lies a copy of T.S. Eliot's Four Quartets. The conversation, which is stimulated by their shared appreciation of the poet, lies at the origin of the friendship and professional collaboration between the architect and the businessman.

Frederick and Laurie Samitaur Smith began their career in real estate investment in the 1970s in northern California, for the most part constructing buildings for the software industry. However, they were never fully satisfied by the formal solutions the various architects they employed came up with for these buildings. According to Frederick Smith, the computer has opened the doors to a new conception of the world, in which a science characterized by non-linear phenomena and the theory of chaos have acquired increasing importance and topicality. Architecture, Smith maintains, especially the sort intended for work undertaken by the operators of the new economy, must reflect this state of things and, as a consequence, be geometrically complex.[40]

In the early 1980s, Smith moved to southern California and acquired some industrial buildings from his father in Culver City. He was ready to take the great leap forward and realize that type of architecture he had had in mind for some time. He only needed the right architect to understand his vision of "a complex architecture mirroring the non-linear mathematics of computer-chip design."[41]

The meeting with Moss took place in exactly the right place and at the right time. Culver City is an area in south-western Los Angeles marked, in those years, by a mix of lower-middle-class homes and small factories, workshops and industrial warehouses of one or two floors, built in the 1950s and 1960s (and some even before the Second World War). These were abandoned in the 1980s in the wake of the crisis in heavy industry and progressive conversion of investments in the production of services linked to IT and the media.

The first commission Smith gave Moss was for a small one-story building at 8522 National Boulevard ("on the wrong side of the Santa Monica Freeway", says Joseph Giovannini ironically),[42] followed by the projects for the Ince Complex at Culver City: Paramount Laundry (1987-1989), Lindblade Tower (1987-1989) and Gary Group (1988-1990), all built, and the design for the Ince Boulevard Theater (1993) from a few years later. Moss's work within the Ince Complex became the starting point for a vast, capillary real estate operation by Smith which sought to convert over 30,000 square meters in a period of about ten years into spaces for the new economy (advertising, entertainment, information, etc.). These initial projects radically transformed the area "turning a 'nowhere' into a 'somewhere'", as Moss said. They also immediately sparked off an efficacious process of revival in the area, in that they stimulated significant political interventions aimed at reorganizing the infrastructure and at improving safety in the district.

Eric Owen Moss has been working with entrepreneurs Frederick and Laurie Samitaur Smith since 1987 to realize a series of projects which, thanks to their courageous urban implications, have the ability to impose themselves within the absent, fragmented space of Culver City. The first series of projects, belonging to the plan called Conjunctive Points, was aimed at two main areas: the Ince Complex (in which Eric designed buildings such as the Paramount Laundry, the Lindblade Tower, the Gary Group) and the National Boulevard district (with over 30,000 square meters of abandoned factories).[43]

A significant project from the early years of collaboration with the Samitaur Smiths is the one called S.P.A.R. City (Southern Pacific Air Rights City) for a park and a raised walkway across the district, linking the various buildings and open spaces. The project follows the disused railway line of the Southern Pacific Railroad which once served the manufacturing and industrial zone and crossed the district, weaving for about a mile and a half from National Boulevard, across the Hayden Industrial Tract and on

S.P.A.R. City Project
(Southern Pacific Air Rights
City)

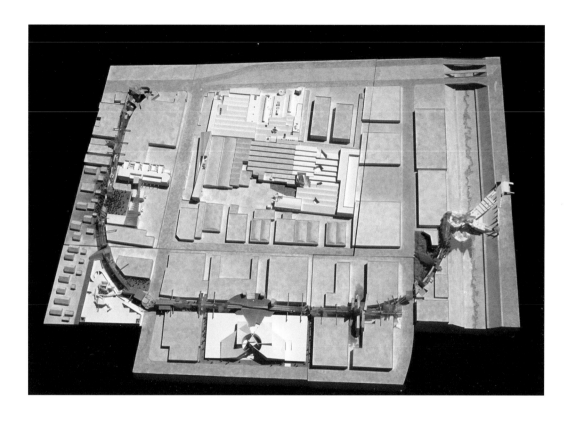

beyond the Ballona Creek. This former railway track, unused now, was nothing more than an element separating the various lots, but in Moss's visionary and appealing project became the basis for a linear green park. Above this park, supported by columns, it would be possible to realize a series of buildings which overlap, rise over and attach themselves to the existing buildings, following but also modifying the plan which, by its nature, is able to change slowly and grow in small increments.

Moss says: "What we are realizing here is an urban fabric in free form which evolves in an unpredictable manner, progressively growing through single operations according to the situations that should present themselves. We are testing a sort of guerrilla-urban planning, a manner of acting on the terms of contingency, which is the opposite of the sort of planning like those of Baron Haussmann in Paris or of Robert Moses in New York. That was a type of planning for an absolute, tyrannical city, born to last hundreds of years; ours, instead, is completely different: it is a way of attacking, uprooting, circumventing, almost dancing in space. The design strategy must be extremely flexible: underlying everything is the ability to improvise and a willingness to change direction, if necessary. This is an urban situation in which some things must be replaced, others must remain, and others may be partially removed."[44]

Following the 1992 riots,[45] international attention turned to other districts of the Los Angeles area than the usual ones (Beverly Hills, Hollywood, Silverlake, Brentwood and Santa Monica which hosted the modernist experiments of the Case Study House program, Neutra and Schindler, but also of the contemporary RoTo, Israel, Morphosis, etc.). One of these was the ambiguous, amorphous context of Culver City, an industrial area located to the south-west which since the 1990s has undergone (and is still undergoing) a general restructuring, under the auspices of Eric Owen Moss and the Smiths.

Despite the proximity to the sites of the riots, the sensation one has on walking through Culver City is not one of threat. Moss's view, as Michael Speaks has declared, is "not the gloomy view of L.A. proffered by left-leaning cultural critics in the 1980s and 1990s"[46] and seems to open the way to new opportunities as far as the urban development is concerned.

The projects for Culver City demonstrate (and this is particularly evident after 1992) the desire to transform the project into a spatial and social workshop. As Herbert Muschamp[47] has written, it is a sort of genetic engineering applied to architecture, an experimentation based on scientific criteria according to which a series of genetically modified buildings give life to a genetically modified city. The then critic of the "New York Times" described Moss's architecture in Culver City not only by praising its artistic quality, although this is present. He is especially highlighting the strategies for survival these projects subtend, which induce a profound and radical metamorphosis of the existing urban structure, thereby encouraging a cultural, as well as social and economic, revival within the stricken post-industrial landscape.

"It is as though it were the materialization of the urban visions of Michael Sorkin and Lebbeus Woods", who in the early 1990s gave form to the almost organic mutation of the contemporary city and also revealed the profound fear that the project was no longer an instrument able to govern these new entities. Moss's projects "exorcise these fears and show the possibilities of contemporary architecture to take root in an anomalous context and to represent it."[48]

International Achievements

"[...] It is Eric's current architectural endeavor that is significant, truly interesting, totally personal and innovative."[49]

"The complex ambiguity seen in Eric's recent formal and spatial constructs has a uniquely probing quality, one that is related to historical precedents in architecture while at the same time clearly an artistic achievement in search of an architecture expressive of the fact that the world is not the way it used to be."[50]

> Saturday 7 September 2002 (Venice, Italy), 11.30 a.m.
> At least a year has passed since the last time I saw Eric. I have not been back to Los Angeles since last summer nor has he come to Italy for a while. We have remained in touch, however, and I have continued to follow his activities. Now I am eager to see him again, to have him talk to me about his latest, gratifying experiences on the international scene. We have decided to meet at the Giardini della Biennale.
> His project for the Mariinsky Theater in St. Petersburg is on display in the Russian Pavilion and this is something he is very proud of, and rightly so. I am extremely curious to learn of the project. How did the commission come about? What is this atypical architect doing in the Russian pavilion? Eric feels like talking. And he does not spare me the details of this work, from the strictly architectural and design details to the more human ones, such as, for example, his conversations with Valery Gergiev, the innovative artistic director of the historic Russian theater. Walking briskly, we arrive at the room containing the model and plans for the project. It is spectacular! Truly, Eric never ceases to amaze.

After having established the most significant part of his professional and biographical development in Los Angeles and in particular in Culver City, the activity of Eric Owen Moss acquired an international dimension with the participation at the Venice Architecture Biennale of 1996[51] which brought him to the attention of the world as a brilliant protagonist. Moss was present in the major exhibition by Hans Hollein entitled "Sensing the Future - The Architect as Seismograph" within a framework that was declaredly open to radicalism and to the most non-conformist of forms in contemporary research. On show were his vigorous projects for Gasometer D-1, Samitaur, Aronoff Guest House and Ince Theater.

However, the most significant and unusual occasion leading to his international establishment took place probably in 2002, the year Moss presented at the Venice Biennale in the Russian pavilion. The presentation of the project for the Mariinsky Theater in St. Petersburg, recently proclaimed the winner of an international competition, comprises the act of affirmation on the world stage, as well as the entry of Moss into the international star system.

It should also be noted that for some time, the Californian architect had revealed his wish for change and a new professional development. As will be seen, Moss's projects began to undergo a significant transformation in the wake of this competition.

"At some point I felt that I had to change how the office represented itself to governments and to agencies and to people who weren't likely to be interested in this office", said Moss after winning the competition. "In order to do that, our purpose was to change the scale of work and the scale of the discussion and to be able to participate (as in the St. Petersburg project and in the Queens Museum project) in different kinds of design and city planning discussions in different parts of the world and to try to find a way to do that which tends to make one more pragmatic and practical, or at least to have that face available and accessible. So I think there's probably not a question about whether this office can make unusual or intriguing objects. I think there was still a question about whether this office could simultaneously solve practical, substantial kinds of programming, organizational and content issues at the same time".[52]

The competition for the reconstruction of the Mariinsky Theater in St. Petersburg ended in 2001. Moss's studio prepared two projects for the two areas set out in the tender, both sharing a common strategy. The first project deals with the restoration and expansion of the Mariinsky Theater which, barely altered since its completion in 1860, has long outgrown its 19th-century envelope; the second one would dramatically transform the New Holland storehouses into a large mixed-use structure dedicated to culture comprising an exhibition center, hotel, museums, retail and restaurants.

Moss was playing his card with the historic city of St. Petersburg, defying its reaction in front of his bold aesthetical choices. He knew very well that his buildings could give the city a shake, and that was his intention. He wanted to contribute, by means of such a strong gesture, to opening up the historical city of Peter the Great to avant-garde architecture and to create a catalyst strategically located inside the urban fabric.

The energetic architectural language, charged with dissonance and courageous geometries, is an expressive gesture typical of the work of Eric Owen Moss: an exploration of complexity and an unpredictable experimentation with materials and forms distinguish all of his projects. What was requested of the designer in this case was in fact that of conceiving an iconic, magnetic architecture for the city; an architecture that, with its strong spatial presence, would be capable to fully express the civic cultural ambitions.

The public, though astounded, initially welcomed the two proposals (one for the new Mariinsky Theater and the other for the New Holland) which were in fact presented to an international audience inside the Russian Pavilion at the 2002 Venice Biennale of Architecture. But over time the new Mariinsky Theater—with its undulating glass and blue-green granite, the unusual combination of existing architecture and new elements, the distortion of the conventional order of spaces—met with the disapproval of some members of the public and of the local authorities. The charismatic "maestro" Valery Gergiev himself, director of the ballet and of the Kirov Opera in St. Petersburg, began to reconsider his position. Gergiev was from the very beginning a strong supporter of the project and even told the news media that "we've got to be radical to attract attention to ourselves". His position subsequently became a little less firm and his latest declarations saw him "support the idea but not the project".

Given the violent reactions stirred by Moss's design and the opposition of local architectural authorities, the Kremlin itself stepped in to ease all polemics and launched a new international competition. In this second phase, 11 architectural studios were invited: five Russian and six foreign. Among the latter were Mario Botta, Arata Isozaki, Hans Hollein, Dominique Perrault, Erick van Egeraat and, once more, Eric Moss. In June 2003, the jury selected Dominique Perrault, to the great disappointment of those who had followed the ins and outs of the competition from the outset.

Following the competition for the Mariinsky, Moss was invited to take part in numerous other international competitions such as one for the Queen's Museum of Art (2001), Grand Egyptian Museum (2002), and another launched in 2003 by the Mexican government for the José Vasconcelos National Library of Mexico.

From the 592 proposals received for the first phase of this important new competition for the National Library of Mexico, the jury selected seven designers for the second phase, including Eric Owen Moss's studio.

The project for the library is new within the vast repertory of projects undertaken by the studio of the Californian architect: although he has produced designs for many public buildings, none of these had hitherto included a library of this importance. The library, like the museum and theater, is one of those public institutions that are sheltered from everyday life. Like churches and temples in the past, this is a place which inspires a sense of respectable solemnity that deserves a privileged position within the city. A national library in particular has the difficult task of communicating and sharing something important and significant concerning the culture and history of a country. The library for Mexico City, especially, was to contribute to the realization of a major national literacy program backed by President Vicente Fox

The proposed project is volumetrically articulated and courageous, but not difficult to read. There is a strong adherence to the functional program, and yet the project is able to transmit all the intensity of the architect's early works. This is not a simple architectural sculpture but a rich, complex construction revealing, once more, a great design maturity.

The library is seen as an extension of the city: the urban grid of Mexico City is transposed into the ground-plan organization of the building, with the pedestrian axis of the Avenida de Los Libros crossing it longitudinally, running parallel to the railway line. The building is thus used to connect to the existing urban roads. The proximity of the railway station, which might have been seen merely as a troublesome hindrance in the planning of a library, instead enters the general design of the complex: the entrance to the library gives on to the station plaza, embracing it (Plaza de Libros y Ferrocarrilles), and the terminal of the Avenida de Los Libros leads the visitor along a route that ends at the railway platforms, framing the moving trains. The four internal courtyards, sculptural openings within the constructed block, are modeled following the course of the sun. To protect from the noise emerging from the station, a hypothesis has been made whereby there will be modifications to the terrain to create an acoustic barrier and at the same time form an amphitheatre which may be used by visitors.

In a certain sense, the building does not fail to surprise us and upset our expectations, though the functionality and respect for the technical requirements prevail. Indeed, while the internal spaces efficiently respond to the logic of the project, the formal athleticism of the volume containing the auditorium thrusting upwards, suspended above the Plaza de Libros y Ferrocarrilles, or the twisted openings of the internal courtyards create a strong, overwhelming effect.

The building reveals a sort of vigorous assertiveness, which well responds to the need—increasingly urgent today, in the face of the dull banality marking so many public facilities—of clearly defining the meaning of places.

Unfortunately, however, the second phase of the competition, which concluded in October 2003, saw as winners the Mexican studio of Alberto Kalach, Juan Palomar, Tonatiuh Martínez, Gustavo Lipkau, with Eric Moss's studio taking second place.

In the same year, the Smithsonian Institution in Washington DC launched an international competition in two stages for the expansion of the Patent Office Building,[53] which today houses the Smithsonian American Art Museum and the National Portrait Gallery. From the 27 architecture studios initially invited to submit innovative solutions for the expansion project, the jury selected seven designers for the second stage: Ian Ritchie Architects; Foster and Partners; Toshiko Mori Architect and James Carpenter Design Associates; Eric Owen Moss Architects; Hellmuth Obata + Kassabaum (HOK); Guy Nordenson & Associates and Pei Cobb Freed Partners; Fentress Bradburn Architect.

The Smithsonian had for some time needed to enlarge in order to provide a home for two museums within the 19th-century buildings: the National Portrait Gallery and the Smithsonian American Art Museum.

The primary goal aimed at by Moss's studio was to ensure the institution would be able, thanks to the exuberance and strength of the expansion project, to display not just the importance of its historic site,[54] but also its status as a major civic and cultural institution.

Once more, the competition brief required a bold, energetic solution, an iconic project that could become the expression of the "city's cultural ambitions". The pragmatism needed to respond in a coherent manner to the need to house the two museums within the 19th-century container led Moss to develop the project in accordance with a scrupulous compositional precision. Thus, unlike other interventions on existing buildings emerg-

Smithsonian Institution
in Washington D.C.
Model

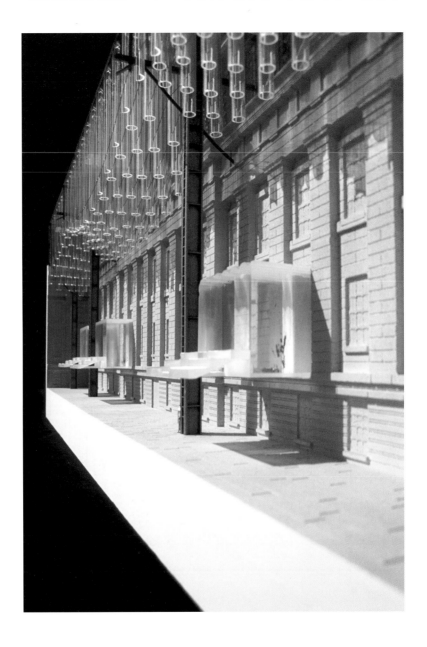

ing from the exuberant hand of Moss, characterized by the presence of new, often irreverent volumes which deform the old structures, Moss here proposed a more discreet and disciplined project, although not lacking in poetic impetus.

The expansion project, which by explicit requirement consisted of enclosing the central courtyard, drew stimuli borrowed from the world of art, offering a variety of spatial experiences. The historic building contains in its interior a spatially rich, welcoming volume which should, according to the designer's intentions, by its simplicity and force confer a wholly unique identity on the institution and so enter the collective imagination. The central court, now an interior with a dramatically spectacular ceiling, could contain up to 1000 to 1200 people. There are many possible configurations of the stage and stalls. The undulating outline of the ceiling over the great courtyard, following a double curve, responds to acoustic requirements and also takes into account the position of the stage on the long or short side of the space. On the upper floor, five of the exhibition rooms extend beyond the limit of the balcony, their glass enclosures overlooking the space below, thus enabling a visual permeability between the various activities that may occur simultaneously in the Patent Office Building.

The simplicity of the typological and distributive conception is matched by a bold experimentation with materials[55] and a technological system enabling great functional flexibility. The covered space of the central court can be transformed, satisfying the demands for changeable spatial configurations of the various programs needed over time.

The project is a lucid and coherent expression of the exploration Moss's studio has undertaken in recent years in the field of architecture as regards spaces for business and culture. Strategies developed for a number of major recent projects, such as the Green Umbrella in Culver City or the New Mariinsky Theater in St. Petersburg, are here implemented in practical terms.

"The competition sponsors [...] expect a visionary proposal," state the contest rules, "one that will distinguish the museum for the next millennium." This is to be expected today, as museums increasingly depend upon their image to pursue clear and long-lasting recognition from the public.

However, by a narrow margin, the jury preferred the project by Sir Norman Foster, who proved to be more academic and controlled; and above all less of a risk, given that he was proposing an already tested solution used for the Great Court in the British Museum, constructed in 2000.

In addition to this intense and energetic design activity, which especially saw him involved in the international sphere, Moss was also nominated as director of SCI-Arc (Southern California Institute of Architecture), the effervescent architecture school to the growth of which Eric contributed from the outset.[56] In his new role, he started moving the school towards interesting new possibilities. Moss has been director of SCI-Arc since February 2002, following Neil Denari, Michael Rotondi and Ray Kappe. Since its early years, the school has stood out for its anti-academic programs and for the non-conformist and often radical approach to its teaching. Moss now has the difficult task of ensuring the school can maintain its original non-conformist spirit and at the same time grow and establish itself even more at an international level.

Moss today is also a figure of clear relevance to the city of Los Angeles, and it is significant that he should want to make the school—which moved to downtown in 2000[57]—protagonist of an incredible opportunity for urban transformation.

In some ways, this is the same dilemma Eric Own Moss himself has to tackle: on the one side, he has to participate in the processes typical of the architectural celebrities on the international circuit, and on the other he needs to preserve his own attitudes that lie at the opposite spectrum of these very mechanisms.

[1] E.O. Moss, *Gnostic Architecture*, Monacelli, New York 1999, pp. 1.3-1.4.

[2] Id., "Which Truth You Want to Tell", in *Eric Owen Moss. Buildings and Projects*, Rizzoli, New York 1991, p. 14.

[3] Herbert Muschamp was architecture critic for the "New York Times" from 1992 to 2004, when his place was taken by Nicolai Ourousoff who previously wrote for the "Los Angeles Times".

[4] H. Muschamp, "Going To See The Box", in P. Scott Cohen, B. Hodge (editor), *Eric Owen Moss. The Box*, Princeton Architectural Press, New York 1996, pp. 56-59.

[5] E.O. Moss, "In the Lexicon of Phobos", in *Eric Owen Moss. Buildings and Projects 3*, Rizzoli, New York 2002, p. 9.

[6] Id., "Out of Place is the One Right Place", in Peter Noever (editor), *The End of Architecture? Documents and Manifestos*, Prestel-Verlag, Monaco 1993, p. 61.

[7] The existence of two moons for Mars (Deimos and Phobos) was hypothesised in 1877 by the American astronomer Asaph Hall, prior to their actual discovery.

[8] See, for example: *Experimental Architecture in Los Angeles* (Introduction by Frank Gehry. Essays by Aaron Betsky, John Chase, and Leon Whiteson), Rizzoli, New York 1992.

[9] "Unlike New Yorkers, who excavated the architectural past for styles and precedents, the young and irreverent Los Angeles avant-garde looked to movies, sport cars, Nintendo games and the ordinary street-side vernacular for inspiration. [...] The buildings were hardly meant to be timeless. The basic notion was not to remake the city in the image of a utopian ideal, but to take parts of [...] "the most deconstructed city in the world" as cues for buildings that do not add up to balanced wholes. If discontinuity is the urban reality in Los Angeles, then it's realistic to design buildings as pieces." J. Giovannini, *L.A. Architects: They Did It Their Way*, in "Los Angeles Times Magazine", May 15, 1994, pp. 30, 31.

[10] The Morphosis studio, founded in 1973, was from 1976 directed by Thom Mayne and Michael Rotondi. In 1991, Rotondi left the studio and started an activity on his own, founding RoTo studio with Clark Stevens.

[11] L. Molinari, *Eric Owen Moss e Culver City*, in "Lotus", 109, 2001, p. 80.

[12] The 1992 riots motivate the strong ideological motivations of their works.

[13] In the spring of 1972, Ray Kappem seven other lecturers and about 70 students abandoned the Cal-Poly of Pomona (California State Polytechnic University) to found the SCI-Arc (Southern California Institute of Architecture) in Santa Monica. This new architecture school immediately stood out for its innovative degree courses and anti-academic specialisations, in open contrast with the more reassuring images offered by the architecture schools of UCLA (University of California Los Angeles) and USC (University of Southern California).

[14] "Perhaps 20 years ago one could talk of a school of architecture in Los Angeles", says Eric Owen Moss, "but not now. Every one of us is working using very different languages. Of course, we cannot deny a connection that links us: the spirit of the city of Los Angeles influences our work; the air we breathe conveys a sense of openness and freedom with regard to novelty. Los Angeles is a very different city to any other and provides the ideal setting for experimentation." E. Giorgi, *Il grande caos di Culver City* (interview with Eric Owen Moss), in "ALIAS" (supplement to "Il Manifesto"), 12 July 2003, p. 4.

[15] L. Molinari, *Eric Owen Moss e Culver City*, in "Lotus", 109, 2001, p. 80.

[16] E.O. Moss, "Which Truth You Want to Tell", in *Eric Owen Moss. Buildings and Projects*, Rizzoli, New York 1991, p. 15.

[17] House of the field watchmen.

[18] A. Vidler, "Beyond Baroque. Eric Owen Moss in Culver City", in *Warped Space. Art, Architecture, and Anxiety in Modern Culture*, The MIT Press, Cambridge 2000, pp. 193-201.

[19] M. Davis, *City of Quartz: Excavating the Future in Los Angeles*, Verso, London 1990; Mike Davis, *Ecology of Fear. Los Angeles and the Imagination of Disaster*, Vintage Books, 1999; Id., *Dead Cities: And Other Tales*, New Press, New York 2002.

[20] E.O. Moss, *What's New?*, in "The

Berlage Institute Report" (*Hunch: 109 Provisional Attempts to Address Six Simple and Hard Questions About What Architects Do Today and Where Their Profession Might Go Tomorrow*), 6/7, 2003, p. 338.

[21] A. Vidler, "The Baroque Effect", in *Eric Owen Moss. Buildings and Projects 2*, Rizzoli, New York 1995, p. 6.

[22] J. Dreyfuss, *An Unlikely Dash of Exuberance*, in "Los Angeles Times", 22 October 1978, part VI.

[23] Richard Meier and Charles Moore, both members of the awards commission, described the project respectively as "a very attractive project" and "unusually spirited".

[24] Moss took a Bachelor of Arts at University of California in Los Angeles in 1965, his Master of Architecture from the College of Environmental Design at the University of California in Berkeley in 1968 and another Master of Architecture from the Graduate School of Design at Harvard University in 1972.

[25] Eric Owen Moss, *Gnostic Architecture*, Monacelli, New York 1999, p. 3.15.

[26] K. Tange, Noboru Kawazoe, *Ise: Prototype of Japanese Architecture*, MIT Press, Cambridge 1965, p. 202.

[27] Moss founded his studio in 1973.

[28] Interview by Leon Whiteson with Eric Owen Moss, 31 January 2002 (www.netropolitan.org).

[29] E. Pound, *How I Began* (1913).

[30] E.O. Moss, *Gnostic Architecture*, Monacelli, New York 1999, p. 1.3.

[31] *Ibid*, p. 1.8.

[32] *Ibid*, pp. 3.7-3.8.

[33] From the project report.

[34] S. Donnell, S.P. Murphy, *James Joyce and Victims: Reading the Logic of Exclusion*, Associated University Press, London 2003, p. 16.

[35] "James Steele Interviews Eric Owen Moss", in *Eric Owen Moss. Architectural monographs, n. 29*, Academy Editions, London 1993, p. 10.

[36] *Ibid*.

[37] Interview by Leon Whiteson with Eric Owen Moss, 31 January 2002 (www.netropolitan.org).

[38] E.O. Moss, lecture "Downtown? Too much is not enough" at the REDCAT in Los Angeles (The Roy and Edna Disney CalArts Theater in Walt Disney Concert Hall) on 12 April 2004, 7 p.m.

[39] T.S. Eliot, "East Coker", in *Four Quartets*.

[40] Laurie Samitaur Smith states: "He was building gigantic boxes and realized when he'd visit the tenants that they were working with a new kind of math that didn't apply at all to the linear spaces he was building. He felt that if we did buildings that were based on the geometries that this new industry was utilizing all day long, they would have a natural—if not conscious, at least subconscious—attraction to this architecture". J. Ringen, *Culver City Renaissance*, in "Metropolis", January 2002, p. 69.

[41] J. Ringen, *Culver City Renaissance*, in "Metropolis", January 2002, p. 70.

[42] J. Giovannini, *Eric in Wonderland*, in "Architecture", March 2001, p. 106.

[43] L. Whiteson, *Packing Up and Heading West*, in "Los Angeles Times", 29 January 1996, pp. E1, E4.

[44] E. Giorgi, *Il grande caos di Culver City* (interview with Eric Owen Moss), in "ALIAS" (supplement to "Il Manifesto"), 12 July 2003, pp. 3, 4.

[45] In March 1991, four policemen from the Los Angeles Police Department (LAPD) beat up a black, Rodney King, who had just been arrested. In April 1992, the policemen were acquitted despite their actions having been recorded in an amateur video. This sparked off a wave of indignation and anger in the black community, resulting in riots lasting a number of days. The city was overcome by a wave of violence with the final tally counting 54 dead, about 2000 wounded and 13,000 arrests.

[46] M. Speaks, *Due architetture recenti. Culver City, California*, in "Domus", 826, maggio 2000, p. 48.

[47] H. Muschamp, "Going To See The Box", in P. Scott Cohen, B. Hodge (editor), *Eric Owen Moss. The Box*, Princeton Architectural Press, New York 1996, p. 56.

[48] L. Molinari, *Eric Owen Moss e Culver City*, in "Lotus", 109, 2001, p. 83.

[49] R. Meier, "Preface", in *Eric Owen Moss. Buildings and Projects 3*, Rizzoli, New York 2002, p. 7.

[50] *Ibid*.

[51] Eric Owen Moss was one of 4 American architects selected to exhibit at the 1996 Venice Biennale.

[52] Interview by Leon Whiteson with Eric Owen Moss, 31 January 2002 (www.netropolitan.org).

[53] The historic building, the former patent office, was constructed in the early 19th century in neo-classical style. It was considered a temple for the industrial arts, and traditionally held the models and prototypes presented by inventors seeking patents.

[54] Walt Whitman defined it "the noblest of Washington buildings."

[55] Glass is used both for structural purposes (engineering consultancy Arup) and for acoustic and lighting effects.

[56] Moss has taught at SCI-Arc since 1974.

[57] Its site at the Freight Depot was inaugurated on 30 November 2001.

Interview to Eric Owen Moss

(Paola Giaconia) The first question I'd like to ask is about SCI-Arc. I read on the "Los Angeles Times" that the school is involved in a trial regarding its property in downtown Los Angeles, and I know there was a first session on May 19th, 2005. What is it about? How did the trial go? Any news already?

(Eric Owen Moss) This is a complicated story if you deal with the details. But I think it's a simple story if you deal with the essentials.

I think SCI-Arc still believes in the tradition of non-tradition. About 4 years ago, SCI-Arc moved into downtown with the intention of buying a big building. The area has become very valuable, and the reason for this is that SCI-Arc brought about 600 people into the neighborhood, and they needed housing, they needed services, and so on.

The result is that a developer brought a big piece of land next to SCI-Arc...

Does your project for the Freight Yard have to do with this?

Yes, it does. That project was with the developer. Together we tried to figure out whether we could get all of their housing and all of their commercial needs, all of the neighborhood's housing and parking needs, all of SCI-Arc's housing needs etc. And we actually solved those problems organizationally.

Unfortunately we couldn't implement the concept legally.

So the developer is now trying to coerce SCI-Arc to support his project. His project requires a "zoning" change, meaning you cannot build big buildings without certain kinds of approvals, and to get those kinds of approvals he needs me to walk into the City Council of Los Angeles and say "I like it". And if SCI-Arc likes it and the neighborhood approves, the likelihood is that they'll get the "zoning" change.

What he is trying to do is buy the SCI-Arc building. Then, if we support his project, SCI-Arc gets its building; if we don't support his project, he'll make it difficult for us.

But you could also not support his project, in which case...

That's in fact the other side of the equation. If he doesn't support us, he assumes we'll make it difficult for him to get the "zoning" change.

And in this context, for one of the few times in my life, I seem to be on the side of the angels. Because SCI-Arc in L.A., and I think internationally too, has a certain kind of reputation. It's very progressive, it's very positive, it's very open, it's very innovative, it's very experimental. And its involvement in the design of the city has increased in a very significant way.

The role of SCI-Arc has changed a lot since it was started by Ray Kappe and then directed by Michael Rotondi. There is a number of people—Thom Mayne, Steven Holl, Peter Cook, Wolf Prix—who over the years visited, and continue to do so. These characters—old, young, in the middle—come to the school, make exhibitions, do books, do lectures, teach... So SCI-Arc is a special place.

And when a developer, with conventional commercial interests, attacks SCI-Arc, I think that in some ways he is attacking a very defensible target.

A long time ago (and I remember reading this), when Stalin was speculating on the various forces in Europe during the Second World War, he made a remark which was: "How many divisions does the Pope have?". It was a sarcastic remark, meaning: the Pope has no soldiers, we don't have to bother with him. So what the Pope did in the Second World War (right, wrong or indifferent) is another discussion, but he had substantial power to influence the direction of events.

Likewise, SCI-Arc has a different means and a different capacity to affect the planning direction of Los Angeles.

So this is the essence of the issue: There is a trial. SCI-Arc may win, SCI-Arc may lose, SCI-Arc may wind up somewhere in the middle. How many divisions does SCI-Arc have?

SCI-Arc is a cutting-edge architecture school and a place that has always nurtured energy and creativity.
Now it has turned into an urban catalyst and a true resource for the city, being capable of triggering actions that occur even outside its boundaries. The role it played in the urban context of downtown L.A. speaks clearly. What can you tell me about your experience in the school, as one of its first instructors and now as director?
My first job as director of the school was first to take the school apart pedagogically, because I think that, in a certain sense, what SCI-Arc started out to do in a poetic way, in an architectural way, in a conceptual way, had been achieved.

I mean design thinking that what was once very marginal, what was experimental, what was questionable, certainly outside of Los Angeles and around the world, has come to be very much accepted...

and recognized, internationally...
Yes! Whereas 10 or 15 years ago people thought all of this SCI-Arc advocacy was either very strange or just peculiar to Southern California. I don't think that was ever true! So critical opinion, whatever it's worth, seemed to just relegate it to something that was local or something that was arcane. The misconception was and is that L.A. is just a strange place... with razor scooters and bubble gum...

a cartoon-like vision of L.A.!
But sometimes those cartoons are effective in dismantling any prospect of seriousness or serious thought. For instance years ago, if I were to show up in New York, or somebody else from here was to show up in New York,

the suggested response was that Los Angeles was never cerebral, thoughtful, philosophical, intellectual, and just had a few people making a few funny looking things.

And SCI-Arc was at the center of that.
I remember... when years ago Peter Cook started coming from London to Los Angeles, and in a way jumping over New York, or Charlie Jencks, or Wolf Prix... and other people who were developing their own critical opinions at that time, SCI-Arc was at the center of that too.
But, as I said, I think in many ways that battle has been won. And it's now a question whether the quality of that work on a large scale can sustain the kind of support that it's now getting.
There was a period of time when the architecture here was in a sense unrecognizable, unacceptable and local. And now it's acceptable and international and recognizable and much lauded and applauded.
And the truth is, I think, that probably both opinions were wrong in a sense. It was wrong initially to dismiss it and to understand it as strictly local. And it's probably wrong now to accept it so readily.

And so SCI-Arc moved from being rejected to being accepted.
Yes, it did over the years. One could argue in a philosophical way whether it's better to be accepted or rejected. This is a discussion that in one form or another you've probably heard: whether it's better to be on the margin or in the center. And if the discourse goes from the margin to the center, has the center come to the margin or has the margin come to the center? I think we're still on the edge.
And the move of SCI-Arc downtown is also related to a reassessment of what SCI-Arc could be.
And this is also interesting in terms of institutional histories. Because SCI-Arc, like anyone young and relatively innocent, was not very philosophical about what it was or why it was or what else it might have been. I think it just was what it was, if you know what I mean. But not very conscious of its role *vis-à-vis* the other schools. Almost inevitably, as you get older, both personally and institutionally, you're more self conscious of your role and your position. And I think SCI-Arc is a more self conscious place now, and in that sense it is more institutional. Because it has an institutional memory now: it remembers what it was, and like a lot of institutional memories it remembers selectively... It forgets things that didn't work and it remembers things that seemed to indicate that it was significant and important.

How have you dealt with that "institutional" memory?
What I wanted to do in some way was to erase that institutional memory. And actually my pedagogical policy was to make a big mess, in a way. To bring in a lot of different people, from Bill McDonald to Lise-Anne Couture to Office dA (Monica Ponce de Leon and Nader Tehrani) to Hernan Diaz Alonzo... young people, middle-of-the-road people. In the first place I didn't want to segregate the discourse on architecture by gener-

ations, which seems almost a convention. You know: the older generation, and my generation, and the next generation. It seems to be a kind of cartoonish way of looking at the world. So I brought in a lot of new people and this involved the school in a lot of raucous debate.

I think in some ways (and maybe this is also true of me personally), I would characterize the work that I did and a lot of the work that was done at SCI-Arc as introverted work, as personal work, and as a kind of working out of private instincts and intuitions about form and space and material etc. And I feel that the international discussion that took place was shared with similar people and in similar places, whether it was the AA[1], or the Bartlett, or Yale... What you had in the end was people who shared common interests talking to each other, and doing lectures, and magazines, and buildings, and all of that kind of stuff.

I believe the discussion now is quite different. The discussion has broadened, the audience is different, the public is much more receptive, and the discussion seems to be now -and I am very interested in this- much less about individual poetry and more about the city and issues in the city and making and remaking the city.

So has the discussion become more productive, in a sense?
Well, it's more ecumenical. It requires a different language.

There were always these public complaints about "we don't know what the hell you guys are talking about. Speak English, or speak Italian. But don't speak *architecturese!*" You know... all of these sort of private vocabularies and conversations. And in some ways that kind of inbreeding and introversion allowed certain kinds of expressions of ideas in architecture to work themselves out. But at the same time it separated that discussion from the larger public. You could argue whether this is good or bad, but the need was felt to participate in the bigger scale of production in order to move these projects from little house remodels in Santa Monica to large scale buildings.

What role did the move of SCI-Arc from West L.A. to downtown play in this sense?
I think the fact that SCI-Arc has moved downtown was very critical because it put SCI-Arc in the middle of a world which is very much changing. And the question is: how will it change?

What are the forces that will change it? And if you look from a slightly longer perspective, whether SCI-Arc wins or loses this current legal fight, what's interesting about it, and I think what makes it a story, is the fact that it is a story about how you make the city. There are really three project areas in downtown Los Angeles.

One is the area around Grand Avenue with Moneo's Cathedral, Disney Hall and so on; one is a little bit further South, around the Staples Center; and one is over on the East side, in the area around SCI-Arc. All of these areas have the opportunity to contribute something organizationally very significant to the way the city is reconstituted.

And if you believe that the city can begin to remake itself by doing so at a number of points (as opposed to growing out of a single center), then the area around SCI-Arc is certainly one of those points, and has very clear connections to the other two. And if you re-imagine that area as the Freight Yard project begins to suggest, this would be a very critical point of departure for re-imagining Downtown Los Angeles.

How can or does SCI-Arc participate in the discussion?
SCI-Arc I think needs to participate in that discussion, which means it has to have a very different voice. So some of the people that come into the school are of course architects we all know, but some of the people now are mayors and city planners and economists and landscapers and so on. And this happens necessarily because the scale of the urban operation requires an exchange of very different kinds of knowledge in a much more ecumenical way.
To give you an idea... An architect called me the other day from Mexico City and he wanted to discuss a project in Baja California. The area is South of San Diego, it's very beautiful and essentially undeveloped, with a lot of beaches and resorts. He wants me to lead a project at SCI-Arc that would study the possibilities of making a new city which combines a resort area with other kinds of infrastructure to anticipate what a new city might be on the Sea of Cortez. So what SCI-Arc is proposing is this: we have a group at Stanford University that we work with (called the Stanford Humanities Lab) and we are bringing in those people... we are bringing in some people from the Universidad Iberoamericana in Mexico City. If you believe that one of the ways architecture moves and changes is to include very different perspectives and information and voices, then... you either have a complete mess and nobody knows what they are talking about or in some way you're able to pull this thing together and direct it and you might produce an unprecedented vision of what an urban/coastal organization might be.

So I guess this would turn into a very special workshop for the students. I mean not for sure a traditional studio project, but an extremely constructive experience that can activate new design mechanisms which are valuable not just for the school, but for the city itself...
This project is likely to involve both faculty and students. I think SCI-Arc is not proprietary. I am not interested in any kind of exclusionary vision of the school. So if Stanford is in, and the Universidad Iberoamericana in Mexico City is in with SCI-Arc, this is ok.
It's more than a workshop. It's a fee-for-services project to produce a conception of a city. And we'll see if we can make something.

Do you think this is one of the directions SCI-Arc might be taking in the near future?
Yes, I think this is where SCI-Arc might be going. But on the other hand we just took down an exhibit of Bill McDonald. A Steven Holl exhibit is going up. We just released a book on Andrew Zago and Monica Ponce de Leon. So we're trying to have double vision, to advance the introverted,

41

poetic SCI-Arc pedigree and to tie that in with broader concerns about the city. Before it turns into an advocacy, before it becomes a formula or a method, I'll leave. I am not interested in an urban mantra. But I am interested in stretching out the discussion and bringing other people in. And you can see now that SCI-Arc talks to the L.A. mayor, SCI-Arc talks to the L.A. City Council. There was a period not so long ago when that kind of discussion would be considered absolutely impossible.

Some people might look at that and consider it a political compromise. I actually don't. If we return to the original metaphor of the margin going to the center or the center going to the margin... I think that maybe the SCI-Arc truth is somewhere in the middle.

What can you tell me about you as a student? What was your experience? Which figures influenced you the most as a young architect?

There were a couple of interesting experiences that I had as a student.

When I first went to college I was probably a little bit too young to know what I was doing (I was 16 years old), and I went to the local school which was UCLA. I was studying Mathematics and I bumped into a teacher, and I always will remember his name: Hans Meyerhoff. He introduced me to a lot of art and literature: Beckett, Kafka... He was absolutely unique and I think he had a lasting influence on me because he opened me up to a lot of very important issues.

Then I was at the University of California at Berkeley. That was a time when Charles Moore was there, Stanley Tigerman was there, Paul Rudolph was there. And there was this very interesting architect who you probably will not know. His name was Paffard Clay.

He had worked for Le Corbusier on La Tourette and Marseille, then he worked for Wright at Taliesin. He had a very peculiar pedigree. He married Siegfried Giedion's daughter. And then he came to San Francisco and he was teaching at Berkeley for a while. He did the Student Union Building at San Francisco State, and the addition to the San Francisco Art Institute (which actually looks like Le Corbusier's Millowners association building in Ahmedabad). I think he had some strong influence on me in a number of ways.

Not so much what he designed, but his attitude towards architecture—which I think was ideal and idealistic... that architecture could both define a life and a personal identity in a world where things are complicated and confusing and contradictory. Architecture drawing a line from the past into the future.

As a matter of fact, I remember talking about Giedion's remark that architecture is a river flowing from the past into the future, and that what an architect does is to drop something into that river and to let it flow on, while of course assimilating things floating by from the past. We're making a book and an exhibit on him at SCI-Arc. A former student of mine from Harvard, who is currently working at Skidmore in San Francisco, is putting it together. Then I studied at Harvard for a while. That experience was complicated. There were some extremely positive aspects. Josep Lluís Sert was there...

And Kenzo Tange also...
Tange was my thesis advisor. That was 1972 or thereabout. The project for the Yamanashi Press and Broadcasting Center in Japan, the one with the big turrets, was very much discussed at that time. He was considered to be an essential character.

Speaking of Tange, what can you tell me about the Ise Shrine and your trip to Japan to visit it?
Tange did a book on Ise[2]. I don't remember reading it when I was at Harvard, but I remember the discussion. That's a fascinating place and deserves a long discussion in many ways.
I think the Ise Shrine has to do with a number of organizational ideas, poetic ideas. It has to do with time, which is certainly a fundamental question whether you're living in a cave or whether you're living on Park Avenue. Here's the concept.
There is a building and it stands for 20 years. Then they take it down and re-build it on an adjacent site. It's a ritual. It's about everything the same, forever, and everything different, forever. Things move and yet they remain the same. They rebuild the building: it's the same building but it's on a different site, it's the same details and the same construction technique, but of course the materials are new.
Change and no change... I mean, it's a contradiction between time and eternity in a way. Or between history and timelessness. And it doesn't resolve that tension. And I think this is the most interesting aspect for me. There's not a belief system that would resolve these contradictions, which are then all expressed in architecture. I think this is actually a wonderful thing.
I came to think that the truth of the matter, the truth of things is not in an allegiance to either the first site or the second site; the truth is in the tension between the possibilities. The Shrine at Ise posits a problem or a fundamental contradiction (the most fundamental contradiction) between change and no change.
The Shrine gets different, it would be susceptible to imagination and to innovation, but, on the other hand, it suggests another voice, which is just continuity. So the tension is not resolved. And that statement is made in the language of material and form and space and function and organization. This is my reading.
I think in the end I am interested in tension. And it isn't so much that I wouldn't like to resolve it... but to find a way to express it.

Speaking of this, of the impossibility of finding preconceived or final solutions to problems... have you ever read Umberto Eco's book Opera aperta[3]? The title in English is The Open Work. Even though the book dates back to the 1960s, I think it has a lot to do with your way of intending cultural production and research.
Also, one of the chapters of the book is dedicated to the poetics of Joyce, an author that seems to be very much present in your discourse about architecture. And in the introduction to the book, Eco says something about

the sense of scientific research and what he thinks it means. He says something like this: "Developing a problem doesn't mean solving it: it can just mean clarifying its terms in order to make it possible to discuss about it"[4].
Yes, I have. I think it's one of his best books. I do have it, and I'm a sympathizer. I met Eco at Harvard on one occasion when I was teaching there...

Do you know that one of his first teaching appointments was in a school of architecture? He taught at the Faculty of Architecture in Florence.
(EOM) I think that's terrific! We should try to get him to L.A.
I won a prize a few years ago which is called the Academy Award in Architecture from the American Academy of Arts and Letters. And what's nice about it is that it has nothing to do with architects. It's much broader so it's given to painters, musicians and even politicians. They gave a prize to Mario Cuomo, for example, who was governor of New York. And Eco got one for literature at the same time.

Getting back to The Open Work, I think one of the messages is that the fundamental issue is being able to articulate the nature of a problem, which is even more important than solving the problem...
I have always been interested in his work, not just because I thought he was so brilliant (because I am not sure he has really any solutions for us). But I think it's, as you say, that what he can do is not so much articulate the resolutions as at least try to put down the issues. Meaning... it's not so much whether he can say what we know, but maybe he is very, very helpful in saying in a very articulate way what we don't know. And that's a step!
To articulate the nature of the problem, as you said... and I agree with you. And that in itself is very, very helpful.
Another thing about the hypothesis of that book is that it suggests that, maybe sadly or maybe happily, you don't resolve or solve. We can only explore. There are syntheses that are momentary, and then they come apart again. It seems to me that, again, the tension between what might be possible, both as things come and go and in terms of the number of ways that you could see or understand, is very much a part of the way I think.
And I think it's very much a part of the way that we work here. I was always interested in putting the building inhabitants or passers-by in a position actually to see and experience in a number of different ways, and not just in a kind of ideological allegiance "it's this and it's not that". It could be this and it could be that!... And I think that's one of the strengths of my work.

How do you think this is understood?
People have talked to me recently about looking and trying to be more, let's say, communicative in a more conventional way, and make the work and the discussion more accessible. I am wrestling with that, actually. You know... Wolf[5] called me the other day and he asked me "when are

you going to become a commercial architect?". And that's a direct quote. I mean, it's a friendly thing to say, in a way, and I am wrestling with that and actually trying to understand how what we do and the way that we work can fit into a context where *misfit* is as appropriate or inappropriate as *fit*. I am trying to figure out how to do it: how to do it in a political way, how to do it in a conceptual way. I think we lost some projects for reasons that have to do with some of these issues... and I am concerned about that because in the end we have to build.

So... do you think it is a problem of communication?
We have several very big projects in the area now, very different and with very different kinds of clients. And I think what I have done is not to make as much of an issue, in concept, of the discussion on the poetics of the building and to make much more of an issue, in a communication sense, on other pragmatic aspects.
These projects are much bigger in size.
We have for example a huge project now for 6000 housing units and 20,000 people. The discussion is a very complex politically, and it will either be done or not done based on how we represent the concept in a social and political sense.
And I think that we have the capacity to design projects of every type and scale. I think what has to be demonstrated is that we have the capacity to administrate and to deal with the public and with clients in a way that makes them optimistic and comfortable and supportive of what we want to do. So that they understand that we are working together, solving problems in a pragmatic, even a prosaic way... and with that will come a kind of special design insight.
I think that's part of the job... otherwise it's very difficult to work on a large scale.

So, how would you explain progress in your work? How have you grown professionally?
Maybe that's the job of people like you...
When I talk to a few people in the profession that are close friends of mine, what probably concerns me about my own work is that, however it looks from the outside, we wouldn't get comfortable and we wouldn't arrive at a method which we would commercialize or sell. And this is not an attack on selling or commerce *per se*.
The idea of looking at a subject in a fresh way or in an experimental way for me seems to be the nature of the problem of architecture and living.
I think the work is in some ways simpler and I think it's clearer now, but I think it still retains its interests in contradictions between possibilities. I think it's stronger, though. And I think what we have to do is to build these big projects...
There has been I think some evolution in political sophistication: working with people, listening to people, and at the same time sustaining a vision about the special place that architecture has to continue to remake

the meanings. This I began to feel quite a long time ago, from Clay and from Tange and probably from my father in some ways too as a writer. Certain things make sense, when from almost any other perspective to me they very often do not. I think there's a softer sensibility in the work now too.

I think it was all very hard edge. I think it was defiant. It had (and has) a kind of instinct for looking at the world and saying: I don't like the way you make your decisions and I want to offer something as an alternative. So I think there was a confrontational aspect. And there's another aspect to it, the other side of the Janus head, which is a sense of withdrawal or retreat.

One is looking at the world and examining the world and in a certain sense defining its priorities and its assumptions, and its villains and its heroes, and its allegiances... and saying: but it should be another way, or it could be another way. And architecture could be that alternative voice. On the other hand, the withdrawal side has something to do with a cocoon mentality that I'm not comfortable with any longer.

What I was referring to, when talking of the early SCI-Arc, was an introversion of sorts... you talk to your friends in your ways about your subjects, and you make a language and you construct a way of seeing the world which is not accessible to other people... I'm past that I think...

... and that only you and your circle of people understand...
(EOM) Yes. And I believe there's something about this which is self protective, and also defensive.

I think you will see this also in your own life over a period of years... that you can grow beyond that... and that that kind of introversion goes away, replaced by a different kind of confidence. And so to some extent the introvert becomes the extrovert.

And it's funny... A client called last night, talking about another architect in a current project that we all have to work with, and was referring to me still as this *enfant terrible* and saying: "the *enfant terrible* has to go and be nice and be friendly."

That's the way we have to do the project.

Anyway... so I think these are the changes that I feel have affected the mentality of the work.

Speaking of your international reputation, which is now very solid and respected, I marked the year 2002 as a kind of milestone in your career. That's the year of the Venice Biennale. You were present at the Venice Biennale inside the Russian pavilion6. That's quite peculiar, isn't it? I find the way your reputation has been made visible to the international public a bit unusual...

I think the first Biennale exhibit we produced was when Hans Hollein was director[7]. Yes, 2002 was peculiar. In my recollection, there had been some serious discussion about exhibiting the Mariinsky project in the international pavilion. And then the Russians seemed interested both in the architecture and the politics of new Russia. So I said "OK".

Мариинку будет строить иностранец

Тайные переговоры в Петербурге

Принято сенсационное решение по реконструкции Мариинского театра. Впервые в истории постсоветской России для осуществления крупнейшего национального проекта приглашен зарубежный архитектор, имеющий статус международной звезды. ЭРИК ОУЕН МОСС (Eric Owen Moss) вчера завершил свой четырехдневный визит в Россию. Перед отлетом в Америку он встретился с корреспондентом „Ъ" ГРИГОРИЕМ РЕВЗИНЫМ.

— Каковы итоги ваших переговоров в Петербурге? Председатель Госстроя Анвар Шамузафаров перед нашей встречей с вами сообщил мне, что проект — дело решенное. Вы подтверждаете это?

— Приятно слышать такое утверждение министра. Раз он так говорит... Проекта театра еще нет. У меня есть идея этого проекта, с ней я и приехал в Петербург, но сам проект должен быть представлен в начале будущего года. 21 января — эта дата зафиксирована в подписанных документах. На сегодняшний день, видимо, можно считать решенным, что мы делаем этот проект.

— Кто его поддерживает с российской стороны?

— Прежде всего председатель Госстроя Анвар Шамузафаров — от лица правительства России. Мариинский театр — это федеральный объект, равно как и прилегающая к нему территория Новой Голландии, которая входит в наш проект. Реконструкция будет осуществляться за счет федеральных средств плюс, разумеется, частные инвестиции. Меня, собственно, и пригласили частные инвесторы, с которыми мы ос

Кто такой Эрик Мосс

Эрик Мосс родился в 1954 году. В 2001-м он, вслед за Фрэнком Гери (Frank Gehry), автором Музея Гуггенхейма, стал обладателем золотой медали общества американских архитекторов, что означает высшее признание в Америке. В Европе Мосс стал известен в 1996 году, когда его персональная выставка представляла Америку на Архитектурной биеннале в Венеции. Основные работы Мосса — частные дома, офисы, общественные сооружения (около 20) находятся в Калифорнии. Это самый «авангардный» американский штат, здесь

— В вашем проекте для театра вы собираетесь использовать этот контраст?

— До определенной степени. Мариинский театр оказывается сегодня мало связанным с ансамблем центральных площадей города. А для гергиевского фестиваля «Белые ночи» их важно связать. На пути между ними оказывается Новая Голландия. Ее можно понять как шарнир, который разворачивает движение вдоль реки в глубь города к театру. В этом смысле Новая Голландия — это именно краеугольный камень. И я попытаюсь выразить эту идею архитектурой, которая должна быть сильной. Мы реконструируем район между театром и Новой Голландией и саму Новую Голландию. Я сейчас не имею права сообщить вам точно, что там будет, но это сильная архитектура.

— Камень вроде пьедестала Петра Великого?

— Нет, не камень. Это будет стеклянный куб, который будет взлетать над водой внутри... Простите, я действительно не имею права рассказывать об этом до 21 января будущего года.

— Стеклянный куб? В ваших предшествующих проектах и постройках вы показали себя как очень авангардный архитектор. Вы попадаете в очень консервативную среду. Вы не боитесь сопротивления?

— Две задачи этого проекта — предложить нечто новое и, с другой стороны, сохранить старое. Это сложный баланс, но работать в таких условиях интересно. Так если вы говорите о консервативной среде города, то ее сопротивление для меня очень интересный фактор, который я обязательно использую в своем проекте. Или вы имеете в виду архитектурных консерваторов?

Sir Winston Churchill made a remark on Russia, saying: "It is a riddle, wrapped in a mystery, inside an enigma." Little did he know he was referring to architecture.

Now, the competition in St. Petersburg was a special case. In Russia we originally won two competitions: we won one for the Mariinsky Theater and we won one for New Holland. There was a lot of criticism, but there was also substantial support. People from the national government (the Russian Federation), and in particular the Ministry of Construction, were very interested in the work and seemed supportive. On the other side was the government of St. Petersburg where there was apparently some opposition. So we'll see how it works out.

Well, St. Petersburg had been characterized as this window on the West...
Yes, the window on the West... On the other hand, it seemed to be in this context somewhat equivocal.
I think that the presence of the Mariinsky project in the Russian pavilion formed what will be a very productive historical debate.

...And then Dominique Perrault won the competition re-run...
By the way, just to illustrate how SCI-Arc operates, I invited Dominique Perrault about a year ago to come to SCI-Arc to give a lecture. He had a big audience, I introduced him and he talked about the Russian project and a couple of other works.

That's very generous of you!
Well, I am not going to win by making somebody else lose.
But I actually thought that Perrault's project was part of an important international discussion.
The Russian government published a book on the Biennale, with a lot of essays on the project, and then they also put out a catalogue on the second competition.
Perhaps I really don't know what is going to happen in St. Petersburg.
The New Holland project is still alive, but we are not working on it now. We just have to be patient, and not jump every time something comes out in the newspaper.
I think, in the end, this Mariinsky competition was a very important experience for me. I think the project is a special opportunity.
I think the international discussion is for me important, and walking along the Neva River is important too.
And hopefully they'll build something.

What do you learn from working in other countries, countries which have different traditions and histories, some of them being charged with a strong historical intensity? Which time do you use as a reference? Or do you rather search through your personal experience for an a-temporal orientation?
I very much enjoy, and continue to enjoy, wandering into various places. I often felt like a sort of nomad, until I actually got married to my pres-

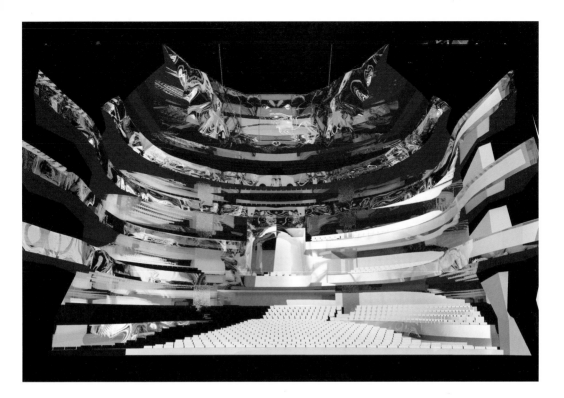

Mariinsky Cultural Center
(version 1), view of the hall

ent wife. I can always remember flying out of Los Angeles and flying into Los Angeles. It's sometimes very different flying away from your home and flying back to your home, but I didn't care much. I didn't feel anything really riveting or compelling in an emotional way about coming back to L.A., until very recently with the current situation: Miller and Emily...

So going out to other places and working and seeing and learning (as long as I don't have to eat fish in Guangzhou...) is something I very much like...
You could have been born in L.A. and I could have been born in Milano. And I always felt that. There is something so accidental about everything. So it's actually wonderful to do all of these things.

Architecture is very personal. You do something and you put it out on the street, and sometimes people throw flowers and sometimes they throw tomatoes...

We were sometimes applauded and sometimes criticized for the Mariinsky project. But I thought that it absolutely belonged to St. Petersburg. That's why I wrote that little piece "To The Ice Sculptors." It wasn't the California architect importing California to St. Petersburg. I never felt that way.

I spent a lot of time in Palace Square and at the Hermitage and going to Dostoyevsky's house and walking around, trying to get a sense of the place.

So it's not my view that I would do what I would do or learn what I have learned in Los Angeles and then run around the world and make copies of that in different cities.

I know that some people disagree, but I never felt that the St. Petersburg project belonged anywhere but St. Petersburg.

The Mariinsky is a very poetic project. And also your text describing the project (To the Ice Sculptors) is extremely sensitive... and very much like a piece of literature. Let's talk about literature and its presence in your work.

What role does literature play in your work and in your research? And what about the other arts (poetry, music, painting, etc.) or science?... I am throwing a few names on the table: Samuel Beckett, James Joyce, John Cage, Henry Moore, Ezra Pound, T.S. Eliot...

I think there's a lot of fake intellectualism in the academy and in architecture, for sure. And not only a lot of fake intellectualism, but there are also fads or trends as you know from your studies. One week it's Derrida and the other week it's Foucault. So there are intellectual trends... that doesn't interest me at all.

When we did the *Gnostic Architecture* book, the book was very much based on Henry Moore. There is a Henry Moore's sculpture called "The Helmet" that interested me a lot. So I constructed the book based on my model of his model of the inside of the outside and the outside of the inside and the glue and so on. It was really just an attempt to try to figure out what was going on.

I had a discussion once with Wolf Prix. We were in a jury together, and we had an argument whether I could ever say anything about Nietzsche or Kafka, because they wrote in German. This is an interesting position for an international architect... that the work could only be understood in the context of the German language.

And I am not saying he was wrong, in a certain way he may have been right.

Somehow these writers give me an insight, or poetry, or a feeling or an emotion. I guess I constructed my life somehow, listening to their voices over a long period of time to try to help me to see and to think and to understand. And there was no particular reason for the selections. My references I think are my own references. I followed my own instincts. They didn't have to do with whether somebody said: you have to read this or that.

I think that those references are somehow helpful to me. They are not things to repeat. They are not things to copy from. And in some ways, if you work on them and use them, they become to some extent not what they are in the abstract, but what they are as you use them to understand. A few years ago we did a proposal for the World Trade Center. One of the images that we used to suggest what we might do comes from a John Cage score.

And looking at the relationship between music and form, architecture and poetry is actually incredibly beautiful and seductive. I never cared for Cage's music, actually... maybe I simply didn't understand it. I had a very difficult time listening to it, and I tried very hard. But the drawings were very suggestive to me of architecture.

For the WTC, we didn't develop a design proposal. It was more a discussion of how you would think about doing a project like that. And the caption on one of our images for the project was a line from T.S. Eliot which said: "last year's words belong to last year's language and next year's words await another voice"[8].

Meaning this was a project America *ipso facto* couldn't understand. It had never done anything like this, it had never been faced with a situation like this... and we were trying to understand something which was entirely new in America's historic experience.

So all of a sudden a John Cage score (I don't know whether he would have imagined himself in this way) came to be used as a conceptual model and a vision of what the World Trade Center could be.

Also Joyce originally interested me. I remember reading his *Portrait of the Artist*[9]. At the very beginning there is an attempt to reformulate the evolving language of a child, as a child goes from its instinct to verbalizing, and the contradictions between those two.

I think that whole issue with language -feeling something and articulating it in words- in a way is not so different than some of the issues in architecture, and this kind of very strange transmutation of form and space, which somehow a client brings to you in words and numbers.

And *Ulysses* always fascinated me because it is one of the most sophisticated and complicated literary structures imaginable. So that it has the appearance of something which is very complicated, if not confusing, and yet it also has a very intriguing underling form and order.

And his work is almost 100 years old now, and we talk about it today as if it were new.

And I think architecture can be like that, and maybe life can be like that... It keeps metamorphosing so that whatever you do, at least in retrospect, never seems quite adequate to say what you need to say, or express what you need to express.

In other words, you are always struggling to find another way to get outside of the rules, of the form, of the order, of the pattern... always finding ways to escape, in a way, to get outside of the outside. The limits are always artificial: a car contains you, a train contains you...

I can always try to get outside of that, but if I succeed, there's always another window, there's always another wall, and there's always another window in the wall... Take our little project "What Wall?"... always a new wall, and always a new opening in the wall.

There's always another limit and there's always another way beyond that limit.

[1] Architectural Association.
[2] K. Tange, N. Kawazoe, *Ise: Prototype of Japanese Architecture*, MIT Press, Cambridge 1965.
[3] U. Eco, *Opera aperta*, Bompiani, Milano 1962.
[4] Id., introduction to the 1st edition of *Opera aperta*.
[5] Wolf Prix.
[6] Eric Owen Moss was also exhibiting in the "A New World Trade Center" exhibit inside the American Pavilion.
[7] "Sensing the Future - The Architect as Seismograph" (1996).
[8] T.S. Eliot, "Little Gidding", *Four Quartets*.
[9] J. Joyce, *A Portrait Of The Artist As A Young Man*.

Proposal for the World Trade Center contest. "For last years words belong to last year's language, and next year's words await another voice."

Form Re-Formed

"I recognize a shape, a space, an organization because I've seen it before. It's in my repertoire, my history, or part of a collective recollection. Alternately, a space or shape is unrecognizable. I haven't seen it. It's new to me. It's outside the collective memory. A dialectic exists between what is previously recognized, and the intention to redefine the boundaries of the recognizable. In other words, how does what is not yet history become history, or how is the conception of form re-formed?"[1]

[1] E.O. Moss. *Buildings and Projects 3*, Rizzoli, New York 2002, p. 11.

Lawson-Westen Residence
1990-1993, Los Angeles, California

The Lawson-Westen Residence is located on an 80' x 180' site, typical of the residential side of West Los Angeles. The clients should be acknowledged because Tracy and Linda had a lot to do with what this house came to be. The kitchen is where they mainly entertain, so that space became the focal element of the building—the place to hang out.

The essential component of the house is a three level hybrid cylindrical/conical volume that holds the first floor kitchen. A cone becomes the roof shape of the cylindrical kitchen, but the center of the cone is not the center of the cylinder. The cone top is cut off creating an ocean view deck. The cone is also sliced vertically, resulting in a parabolic curve. Pulling the curve toward the street lends rise to the vaulted roof. The original scheme for the building had three rectangular plan elements, the residue of which appears sporadically in the final kitchen section. Linda will come in and ask, "Why is this piece of the kitchen over here?". And the answer is that it is from the scheme that is not here anymore. So there are obligations to a building that never was.

This project inclined toward conceptual dissection—toward taking apart buildings at both a large scale (walls and roofs), and the next scale down (doors and windows), and further still (screws and washers). But there is also a way to re-assemble the pieces. Apart and back together. Both.

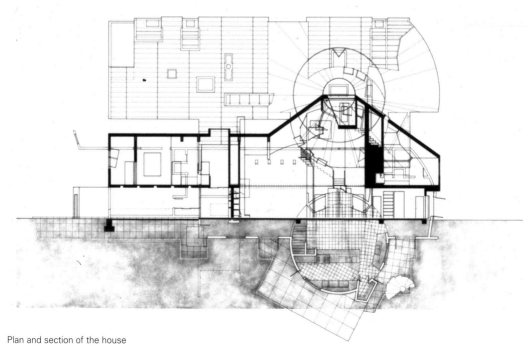

Plan and section of the house

The back yard

Street elevation

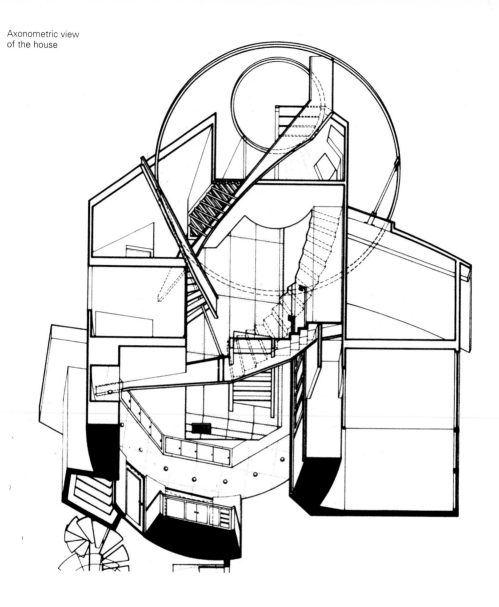

View of the house from
the gate

View from below

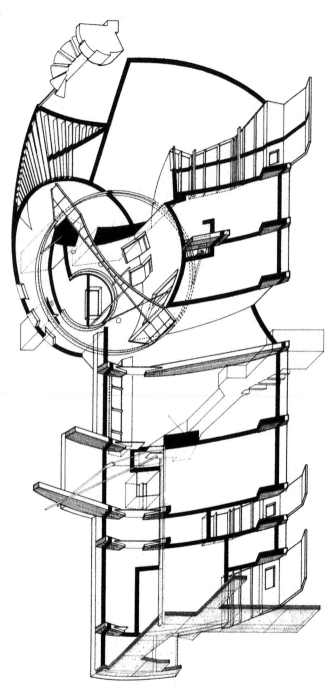

View down to the kitchen

Aronoff Guest House
1991, Tarzana, California

The existing house is a nondescript tract house on the northern side of the Santa Monica Mountains. The property stretches north-west of the existing house and down a slope to the Santa Monica Conservancy, a beautiful wooded area extending for several miles, protected in perpetuity from development.

The new guesthouse is a pleasurable toy for its owners, their employees, guests, and children. The building can be climbed on, examined, and used as a viewing platform.

The project—combining studio, office, and a private apartment—is positioned at the transition from flat to sloping portion of the site, adjacent to the south-west property line. The position of the new house on the site also allows clear visibility and access from the street for those who come to it directly to do business.

The project contains three floors: the top-level studio/executive offices for the owners; an office floor at grade for a business with three employees, and a separate apartment below for an elderly father. The roof,

designed as a stepped bleacher/deck with open and covered areas, is oriented to the view of the Conservancy area and the San Fernando Valley. It is accessible from all levels via a stair that runs along the perimeter of the house. It is also accessible internally, directly from the third floor.

The middle (grade level) is the office floor for three employees, used during the workday in conjunction with the owner's office on the top floor. The apartment at the lowest level has elevator access, a covered deck area, and an open patio. All levels may be accessed from the middle level lobby or from the exterior.

Rather than stacking floors as a building steps to acknowledge a hillside profile, the guesthouse emerges from a conical cut dug at the edge of the hill. The project—secured at the edge—combines sphere and cube, neither quite legible.

So... placed precariously at the top of a slope; stabilized by the conical cut; a threat to roll as a sphere; re-anchored by the cube—the guesthouse—a stable instability.

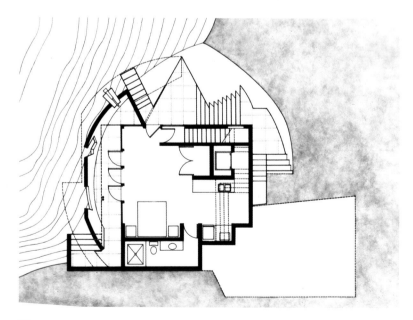

Ground floor plan

Model

Section model

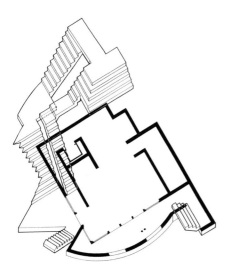

Ground floor axonometric

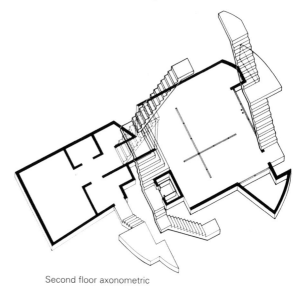

Second floor axonometric

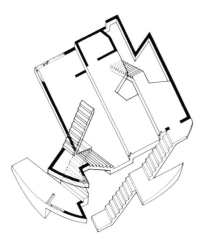

Third floor axonometric

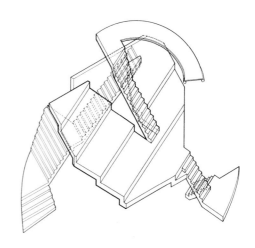

Stair configuration

The steel model

Aronoff Residence
1999, Calabasas, California

A 26 acre Santa Monica Mountains top site adjacent to the Mulholland scenic highway has a building pad, roughly 1000' x 60', which is the result of a previously planned development which never proceeded beyond the grading.

The owners offered a complex building program which included a main house for a family of four, office space for a staff of eight, a guest house, a two unit grandparent's house, gardens, recreational space including a tennis court, pool and pool house, an amphitheater, and an entry gate station. A two lane on-site road, positioned north of the buildings, provides entry and egress for a 25-car underground parking structure.

The Mulholland Highway is designated a "scenic corridor", so criteria setting building dimensions, relationships between building and land, and visibility from the highway is monitored by the local planning agency.

The project is an exploration of an archetypal building problem: how to build at the top of a mountain site. The fundamental visual intent from the earliest sketches and models is to produce a delicate, "un-building-like" profile stretched across the top of the mountain—clearly not a natural feature, nor recognizable as a conventionally made object.

Viewed from the road, the hilltop will not appear as a well-protected enclave, nor does the project design posit man and land as adversaries, contesting for control of the mountain. Building is still building—visually discrete; land is still land—visually discernible. And yet the two inform each other. That is, this building was meant for this hill; this hill for this building. That is the intention.

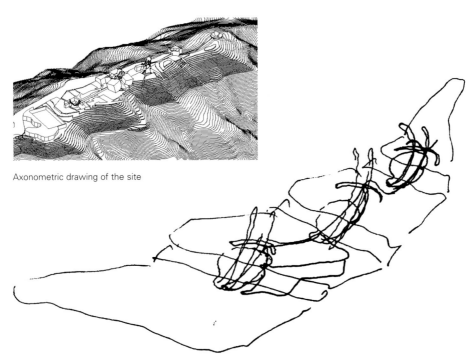

Axonometric drawing of the site

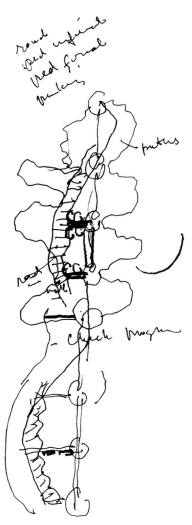

Sketch by Eric Owen Moss

View of the model down
the main axis

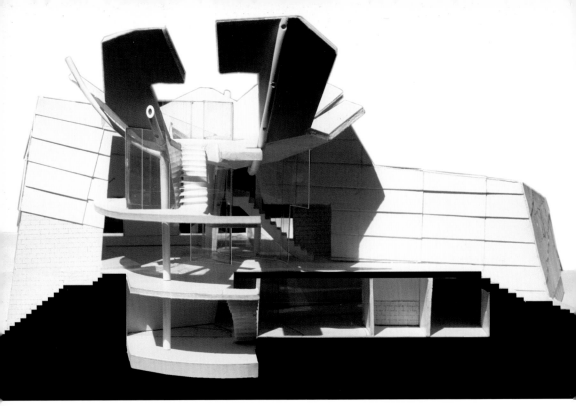

Model of the main house

West and South elevations

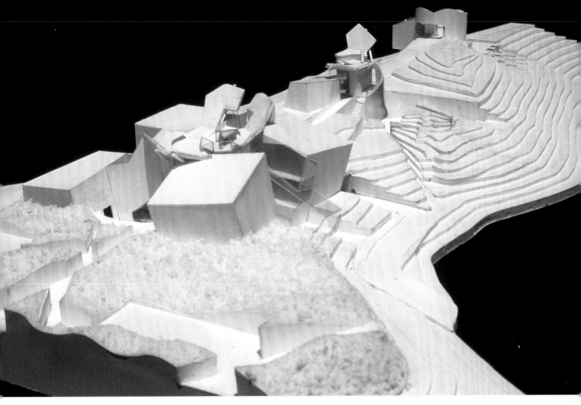

View of the model
and the site

Gateway
2000-, Culver City, California

The 3505 Hayden Avenue project is located at the southwest corner of the National Boulevard and Hayden Avenue intersection. The project contains approximately 175,000 square feet of office space on three levels and a 300,000 square foot parking garage with 778 spaces on four subterranean levels.

There are two critical site features. First, the project adjoins National Boulevard, a major north-south Los Angeles thoroughfare. The curving northwest elevation of the building is prominently in view for this high-speed traffic. Second, the corner of National Blvd. and Hayden Ave. is a prominent automobile gateway to Conjunctive Points, a group of new commercial and performing arts facilities.

The regularity of the office design is intentionally interrupted by a "coil." The coil is a three-story, 45-foot diameter, poured-in-place concrete tube, "reformed" as a consequence of various programmatic requirements so that it is no longer a literal tube. The coil is divided into three aligned but disconnected segments which imply that there was once (perhaps) a single tube. On the National-Hayden corner, the tube lands vertically, emphasizing the importance of that street transition and encloses entry, stairs, and balconies. The second section faces Hayden Ave. and bridges the office building wings, spanning a large water feature below. This section contains stairs, bridges, balconies, a conference center and a café. The third portion of the coil opens to a landscape garden and the tube lands at the south end of the project. Half of the coil is enclosed to hold a large, convertible conference and multi-media center.

The curved northwest building wall also breaks the regularity of the typical office floors. The wall combines a series of third floor bleachers, offering spectacular city views, with intermittent service/utility towers extending from the below grade parking area through the office floors above.

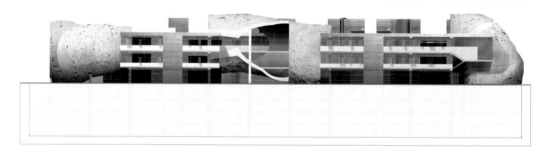

Elevations

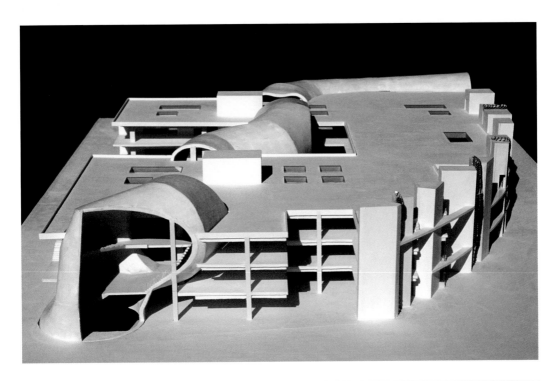

Study model

Animation stills

Control lines

Study model

View from Southwest

View from Northwest

The Charm of the Unknown

"I'm intent on constructing the conflict between [...] what is recognizable as an existing type, known to history, and a pre/post historic postulate which suggests that the form itself is not static."[1]

[1] E.O. Moss, *Buildings and Projects*, Rizzoli, New York 2002, p. 9.

Samitaur Complex: Phase 1
1989-1996, Los Angeles, California

The design for this office building utilized the air rights over a service road to create space in a dense existing fabric. The new structure is elevated fifteen feet—the required clearance to maintain vehicular access—over the service road and ties the extant buildings together into an office and classroom complex for a digital imaging firm. The building in the air is conceived as a simple rectangular block supported by steel pipe columns and girders that span the road.

There are two design exceptions to the block. First, the entry/exit stair and lounge/roof deck space on the southeast corner where cars enter the site and second, the west-facing courtyard area with bridge, pool fountain, and employee outdoor seating, that hangs over the auto egress road below.

The interior of the Kodak Building is laid out as an open plan to accommodate the varied programmatic requirements: open and closed office space, conference rooms, multimedia classrooms, lounges, cafes, and raw production space.

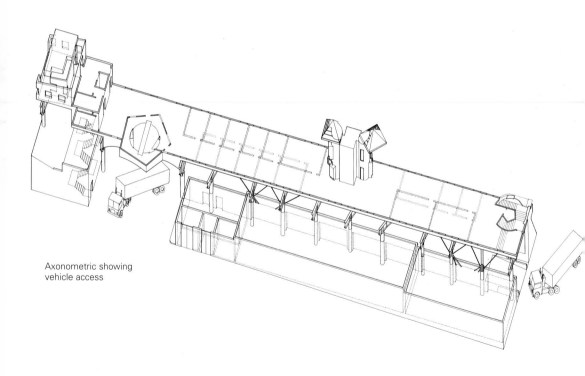

Axonometric showing
vehicle access

View from Southeast

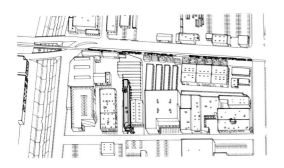

Site plan

View from Northwest

Structural axonometric

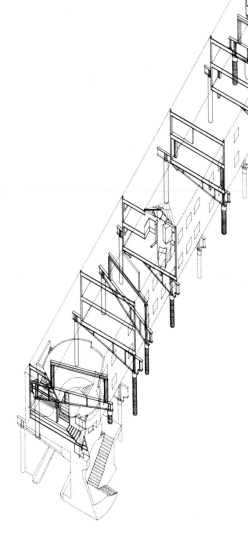

View from Southeast

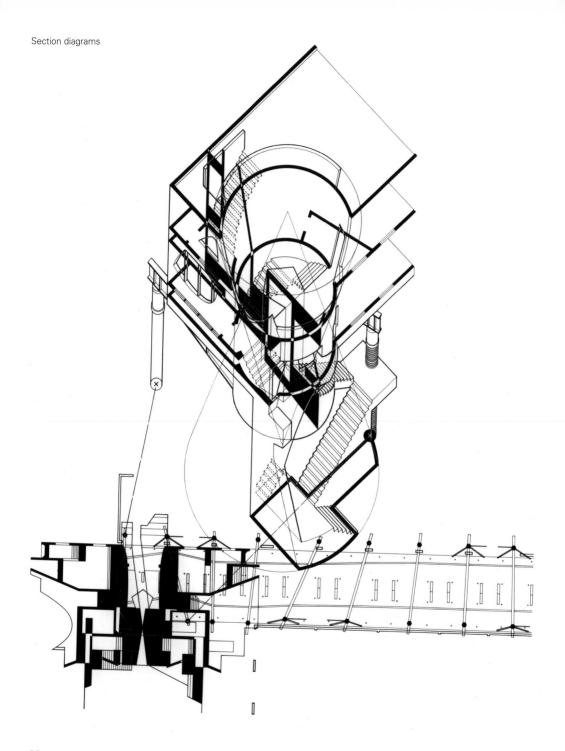

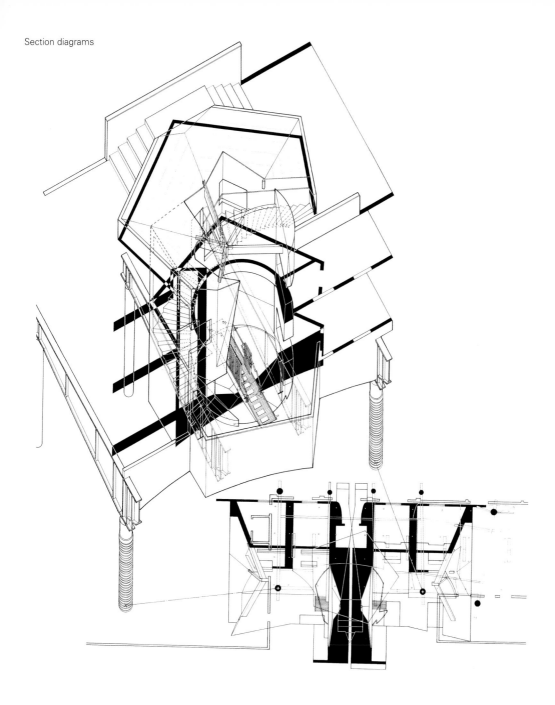

Exterior bridge

Aerial view of exterior terrace

Samitaur Complex: Phase 2
High-rise Towers 3a-3b (Jeff-Jeff Towers)
1997-, Los Angeles, California

The site is highly prominent, rising out of a corner created by a sharp turn on Jefferson Boulevard and is adjacent to the Santa Monica Freeway and La Cienega Boulevard, a major thoroughfare.

Support from the Los Angeles Mayor's office has led to a major change in the general plan for this site, most notably a lifting of the height limits. These towers rise out of an existing saw-tooth warehouse that will be completely renovated to become the street level circulation between the new buildings, as well as space for retail and commercial development.

The office space itself is not typical. The larger floor to ceiling heights (22 feet) are designed to create a loft-style feel, an atmosphere less constraining than the usual tower project and more appropriate for the type of tenants anticipated, design and production companies. This also gives these tenants the possibility of adding mezzanine levels.

A steel column grid supports the major structural load of the building with steel bracing expressed on the facades carrying wind and seismic load.

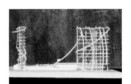

Views of the model

Control lines

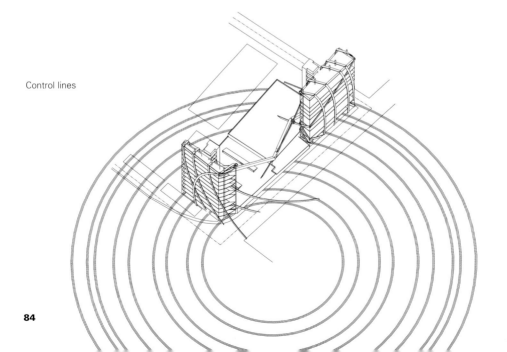

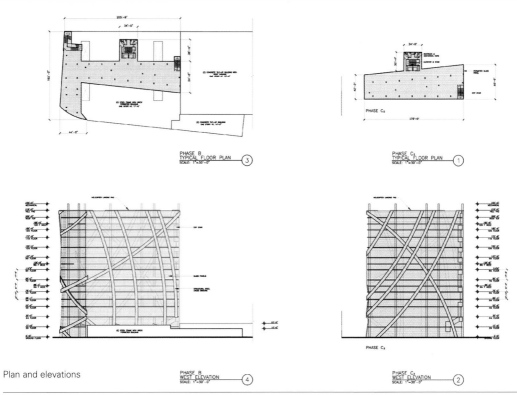

PHASE B
TYPICAL FLOOR PLAN ③
SCALE: 1"=30'-0"

PHASE C₂
TYPICAL FLOOR PLAN ①
SCALE: 1"=30'-0"

Plan and elevations

PHASE B
WEST ELEVATION ④
SCALE: 1"=30'-0"

PHASE C₂
WEST ELEVATION ②
SCALE: 1"=30'-0"

Perspective

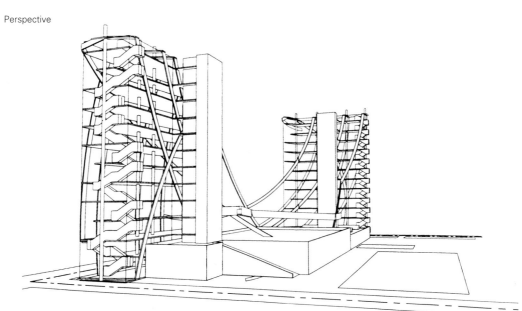

Ten Towers
1991-, Culver City, California

The Ten Towers project occupies a three-sided property with street access from the south. The triangular site is filled with a single story 14-foot clear loft with a parking roof deck above. Auto access is up an entry ramp to the parking deck with stairs/elevators to the building's interior. In the central area of the site, a ground level public plaza offers seats for outdoor performances, or simply lounging, sitting, or sunning. Pedestrian entry is through this plaza then directly into the building.

What is conceptually unique in the project design are the ten towers. The concept juxtaposes two distinct building types. The first type involves nine "towers" that project vertically forty-two feet above the parking deck. The towers are constructed of masonry on the "exterior" of the site and glass on the "interior." Wherever the surface does not conform to the parking grid, holes are cut in the roof structure to form open light courtyards for the ground level offices. Black bamboo is planted directly behind the translucent glass, moving in the wind as if silhouetted on a glass screen. Though all nine towers are simple shapes, their plan forms vary significantly from one another, so they are perceived both as discrete shapes and as a complex grouping of variously sized objects.

The tenth tower—the second building type - is not quite a simple geometric shape, but rather a gently twisted ex-rectangular volume. A vestige from a former scheme that placed the tower in the same location as an existing steel frame tower, the tenth tower contains three floors of office and conference space. The tallest of the towers, the walls are made entirely of vertical and horizontal glass louvers and vision panels. Where sun orientation or restricted views occur, a grid of blue, obscure glass intervenes in the tower wall. The intention is not to suggest a preference for one shape or the other but to present the interrelationship of two design topologies that rarely occur within the same project.

Perspective from South

Proposed construction

Existing site and buildings

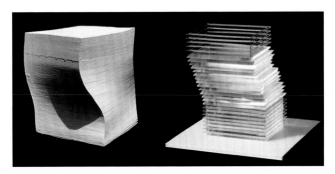

Concept models

Plan view

View from North West

Architecture vs. Itself

"The earlier work investigated overlapping geometrical entities. Then the interior space—Western. Now it's the space between inside and outside where geometries dance. The space in between is flexing. The inside of the outside and the outside of the inside."[1]

[1] Eric Owen Moss, cit. in "Beyond Baroque. Eric Owen Moss in Culver City", in A. Vidler, *Warped Space. Art, Architecture, and Anxiety in Modern Culture*, The MIT Press, Cambridge 2000, p. 193.

The Box
1990-1994, Culver City, California

An existing industrial warehouse was renovated to contain new office space. The Box, located on the roof of the office, became a private conference/meeting room and explores the process of inserting a new building into an existing structure. The Box serves as an identifiable architectural element or event along what was then a relatively non-descript street elevation.

Pragmatically, the Box has three parts. The first is an almost cylindrical reception area, which extends upward and cuts the roof of the existing warehouse. Behind the reception area is an exterior stair leading to a second level roof deck, supported on the exposed truss system below and suspended over the cylinder. Up the exterior stair is the Box itself, a private 3rd floor conference space with corner views west to Century City and east to downtown L.A.

The windows in the Box are purposely positioned high to prevent seeing the street below and direct the views toward long vistas of the trees and sky. The entirely of the Box is an almost black cement plaster inside and out. Roof, walls, and ceilings are a consistent surface. No material distinctions are made from roof to wall or from interior to exterior.

The box is supported on steel legs formed around an imaginary globe. The residue of the globe is manifest in the arched beam profiles and two curved steel channels which tie the beams together. The intent was to produce a kinetic architecture—the box precariously sitting on a sphere.

Sketch by Eric Owen Moss

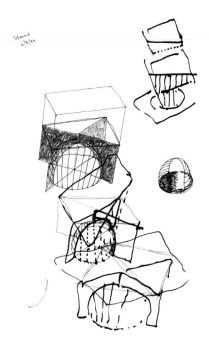

Sketch by Eric Owen Moss

View from the North
along National Blvd

Plan diagrams

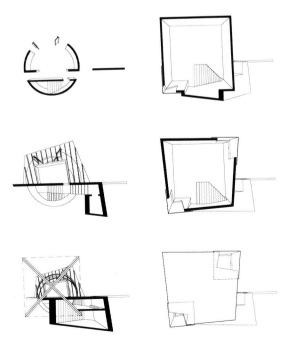

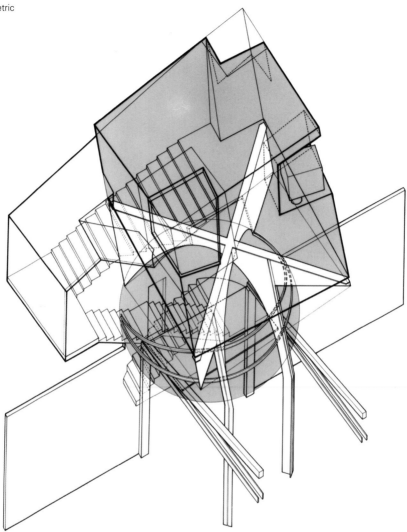

View from the East

The Beehive-Annex Conference Center
1996-2001, Culver City, California

The Beehive is a new office building and conference center that was inserted into an existing fabric of warehouses. An existing two-story, dilapidated wood building was removed and a new two-story structure was designed over its same footprint. The site is captured on three sides by existing buildings, leaving only approximately 35 feet of public street façade. The project is an exercise in creating a public image of a building, capable of communicating its presence along a busy street elevation. The front portion of the building, referred to as The Beehive, was the solution to this problem.

The Beehive and the adjacent buildings are set back from the street to create a garden plaza which will eventually house a coffee bar and allow workers in the entire complex to meet.

The shape of the Beehive was dictated by programmatic requirements and the constraints of the site. The varying shape responds to the different internal functions and the act of attaching to an existing group of buildings. The structure is in essence, four columns that are wrapped horizontally by tubular steel at four-foot intervals that provides the framework for the exterior cladding. Had nothing else been done to the structure, the final shape would have been a cylinder. The horizontal structure is clad using a shingle system of glass planes or thin sheet metal walls that is expressed on both the exterior and interior of the building.

The ground floor of the Beehive is the main entrance and reception area. A stair leads up to the second level conference center for the company. Another stair leads outside from the conference center and forms the roof of the Beehive. The stair triangulates around a pyramidal skylight that lights the conference room below. A roof terrace provides spectacular views of the city and a space for small informal gatherings. Stairs rise to the roof. Stairs are the roof.

Sketch by Eric Owen Moss

Site diagram

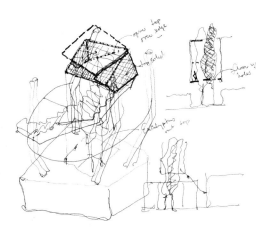

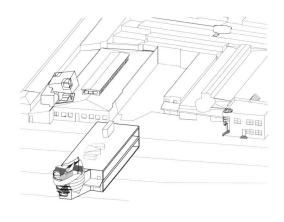

View from the garden

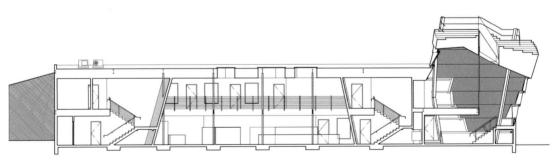

Longitudinal section

What Wall?
1998, Culver City, California

The original site was part of an existing sawtooth warehouse in a former manufacturing zone. The requirements for the new tenants, a software design company, included office and conference space, computer facilities, and open areas for informal interaction.

The expressive feature that gives the structure its name is the 30'x30' wall that makes up the front of the building. The wall is constructed from one thousand 8"x8"x8" concrete blocks. Each block had to be specially cut and connected, wired into a complex pipe structure that supported the blocks. Three steel windows interpenetrate the undulating form of the wall. Deceptively simple, the wall required 52 working drawing sheets to produce the windows alone. This front element of the building serves as a constantly changing surface that functions in counterpoint to the extremely regular lines of masonry.

In the back work areas the renovation was more minimal. A central interior courtyard punctuates the two-story space. The open space is easily accessible to all the offices and facilitates the company's constant collaboration.

View from the Southwest

Site plan

Aerial view of roof

View from below

Recollecting Forward

"[...] Time present and time past
Are both perhaps present in time future.
And time future contained in time past
[...]"[1]

"[...] history is running in both directions
[...]"[2]

[1] T.S. Eliot, "Burnt Norton",
in *Four Quartets*.

[2] E.O. Moss, *Gnostic
Architecture*, Monacelli,
New York 1999, p. 15.

Pittard Sullivan
1994-1997, Culver City, California

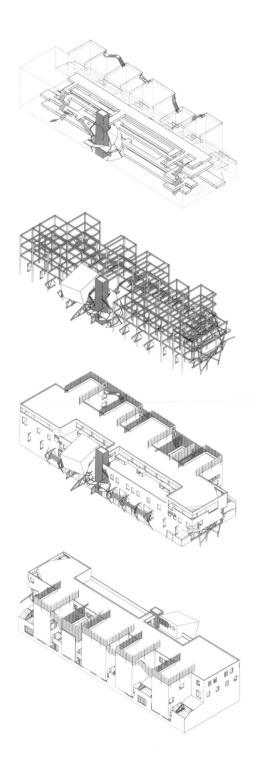

3535 Hayden Avenue is quite literally a building built over a building. Originally the site held a group of old industrial structures. All were demolished with the exception of the wood double-bowstring trusses, post supports for a warehouse roof and a masonry wall that ran the length of the site. A four-story steel frame—tube columns and wide flange beams—was positioned over the original wood structure. The interest was to create unusual spatial possibilities that were the result of the amalgamation of two structural systems that do not usually co-exist. Interior spaces express elements of both construction systems and both the wood trusses and brick wall are visible from the exterior.

The building tenants—a multimedia graphics and advertising company—were interested in having a building that was visible and accessible to both visitors and employees. It was important for them that people see and would be seen to encourage an open and interactive work environment. This philosophy directly affected the design of the lobby. All of the circulation systems—stairs, elevators—accessed from the lobby are glazed. Bridges traverse across the three-story lobby at all levels, providing various vantage points to the lobby and to glazed office spaces. The building was organized around a circulation/exhibit gallery, designated by the location of the old wood posts, which runs the length of the building and can be accessed from the central lobby.

The ground level includes a cafeteria and dining area with access to an outdoor, enclosed garden. Open design and production areas on the ground floor take advantage of the unusual spaces formed by the intersections of steel frame and wood trusses. The second and third floors are a mix of editing bays, state of the art computer rooms, galleries, a large library, and private and open office spaces. At the forth level there are the executive offices which are set back on the south side to create a large outdoor deck and lounge.

Component diagrams:
circulation; structure;
complete from the
South; complete from
the North

Site plan

View from the Southeast

View of the entrance

Elevation on the parking

The louvers in the back

Central lobby circulation

Wedgewood Holly Complex: Green Umbrella
1996-1999, Culver City, California

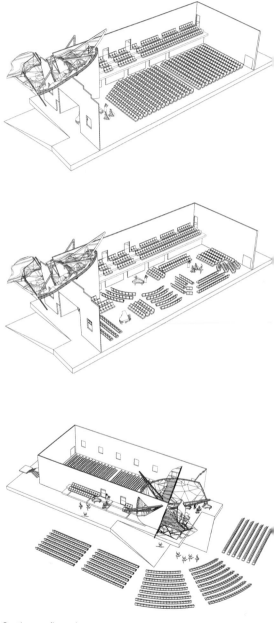

The Umbrella was originally designed as an outdoor performance balcony for the "Green Umbrella", an experimental series put on by the Los Angeles Philharmonic Orchestra. The fundamental design intention was to provide a venue for a small number of musicians (5 to 10) who would perform on the balcony for an audience seated below. The Umbrella itself is a cascading series of laminated glass panels mounted on a steel structure over the open-air platform and stairs. The glass was arranged to both shelter the musicians and enhance them acoustically.

The interior was designed to accommodate numerous different performance arrangements from multiple small venues to a 30 to 40-person orchestra. When the tenants changed, the Umbrella continued to function as a bandstand for musicians or speechmakers as well as a lunchtime seating and roof deck/lounge area. The Umbrella has become a favorite local venue for public events.

Site plan

Seating configurations

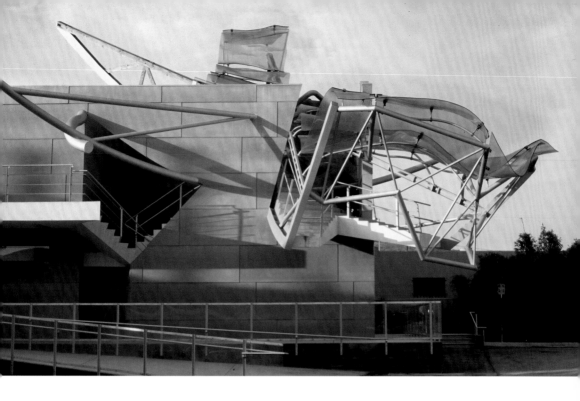

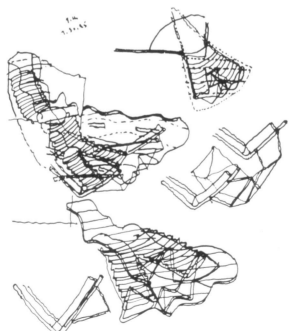

Sketch by Eric Owen Moss

Following pages:
West elevation

View from the corner

Exploded axonometric view

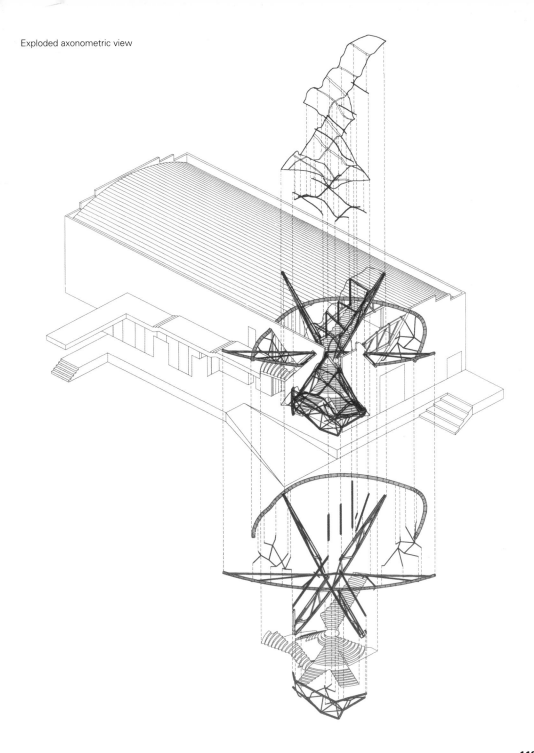

Wedgewood Holly Complex:
Slash e Backslash
1998-1999, Culver City, California

The two office buildings were originally part of an un-interrupted fabric of wood frame truss roofed warehouses that had been added to sporadically since the 1940's.

The design strategy involved a "Haussmanization" or strategic removal of the original agglomeration of buildings to arrive at the final configuration of the buildings. Based on the required square footage and the existing structure of the buildings, the old construction was cut out, demolished and removed. An open space was created between the two buildings to accommodate on-grade parking.

The front elevations are glazed where the existing buildings have been removed in a "single slice". These inclined glass facades allow the interiors to flow into the garden space, visually connecting the buildings with the plaza.

The slice exposes the original wood structure in an unusual way. Where the now sliced roof was structurally inadequate a series of new steel pipe supports and braces were added within the façade.

The interiors are large, open, flexible warehouse areas, lit by skylights, which have been filled with a variety of program uses. A new steel frame was introduced to deal with lateral loading and steel supported mezzanine floors were designed to accommodate additional program space. The buildings form the northern edge of a campus-like garden plaza.

Axonometric of Backslash

Slash axonometric

View through sloping glass

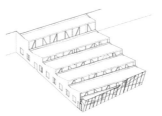

Slash and Backslash

Wedgewood Holly Complex: Stealth
1993-2001, Culver City, California

Three existing contiguous warehouses in an old industrial/manufacturing area in Culver City that at the time was largely derelict and unoccupied were planned to be converted to offices that would attract a new type of tenant who was less interested in the usual amenities of commercial space, such as a downtown location or conservative building type, and more interested in the technical infrastructure of the building and a stimulating work environment.

In the warehouse closest to the street, chemicals used by a former tenant had leaked out over a number of years and contaminated the soil beneath it. The first warehouse was demolished in order to gain access to the substandard earth. That earth was removed, leaving an enormous cavity. Rather than filling the hole, it was reshaped to form a large outdoor theatre/garden with seating for 600. The new building could not exceed the square footage of the building that was removed and had to comply with the local height restrictions. The ground was kept clear to allow for the client's requirements of the garden and on-grade parking so the building was essentially lifted in the air. The entire structure, 315 feet long and 56 feet high, is separated from the two existing buildings on the site by a masonry wall. The first step in the design was to span the newly formed outdoor theatre/garden at the north end of the site. This was done with 75-foot trusses that clear span the garden and are supported on either end by steel tubes. At the south end of the building there is a large opening in the masonry wall that provides pedestrian and auto entry/exit access through the Stealth to a campus-like site in the rear.

The ground level of the complex on the east side of the masonry wall was renovated to hold a 200 seat theatre that opens to the sunken garden, open and closed office space, and conference/meeting rooms for the Ogilvey & Mather advertising firm.

An essential idea of the building is not to produce a single shape but rather an evolving section over the length of a building. The transformation in section from a square to a triangle provides a constantly varying sequence of interior and exterior spaces.

Site plan

Structural diagrams

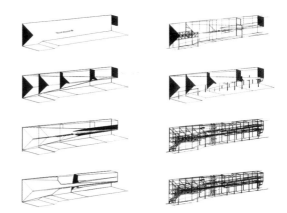

Axonometric

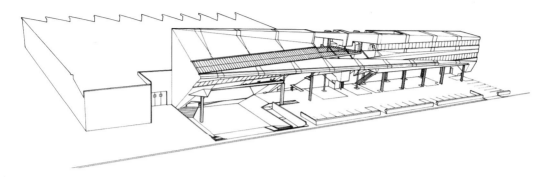

Structural frames

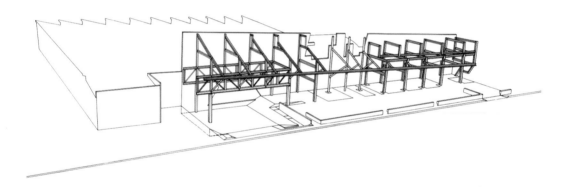

North concrete block wall

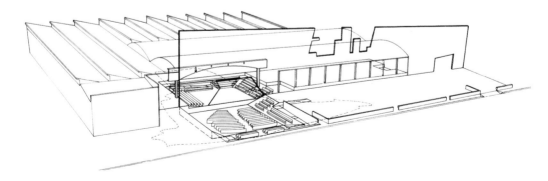

Amphitheater with doors
open

Transverse section through
amphitheater

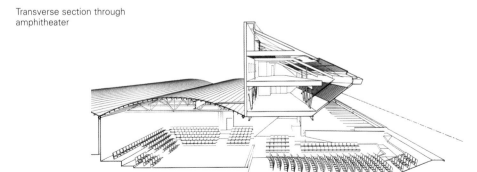

Ground floor lobby

Main space with clear span

Wedgewood Holly Complex:
Parking Garage e Pterodactyl
1999-, Culver City, California

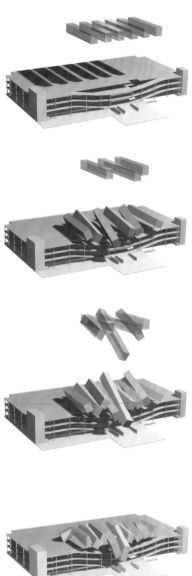

The Pterodactyl explores a hybrid program of an office building/parking garage, allowing the former to obviate the presence of the latter.

The four-level parking structure is straightforward and inexpensive: steel frame, metal decks, regular bays, and ingress/egress ramps attached at opposite ends of the public face. The 600 space capacity structure serves as a podium for a rooftop office building. Because buildings in the area are three floors or less, the parking structure roof affords spectacular vistas of the entire city from downtown to the Santa Monica Mountains to the West-side of Los Angeles.

The office space is formed by the intersection and manipulation of nine elevated rectangular boxes. The boxes are supported on the steel column grid of the parking structure, which in anticipation of the office building construction, have been extended two levels above the fourth floor deck.

Site plan

Massing diagrams

Structural model

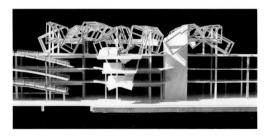

Montage view from Southwest

Model

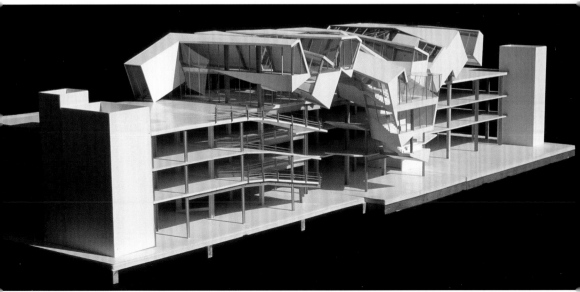

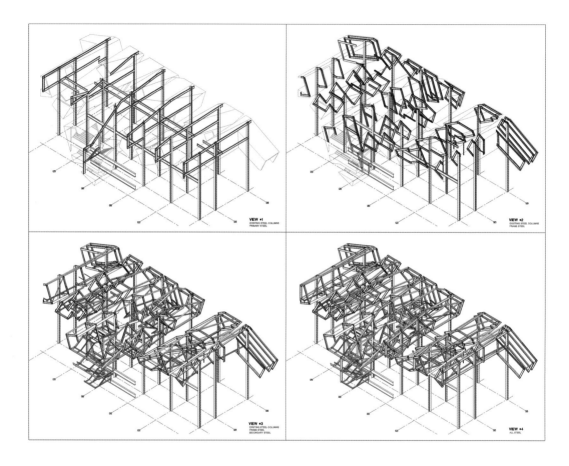

Model

The Spa
2000-, Culver City, California

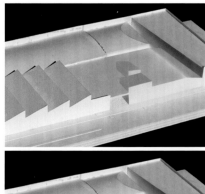

The project is a health club designed to accommodate the exercising and relaxation needs of a growing number of neighborhood professionals, and those of the students and teachers at an adjoining ballet studio. The neighborhood is a dense collection of mostly one story industrial structures. The proposed health club/spa is inserted in the existing complex by removing a portion of the existing ex-industrial fabric, replacing it with a new three story construction, then re-connecting the existing ballet studio with the new club. The street level floor holds gym space, a health food bar, and men's and women's spas and dressing rooms. The second level includes a number of treatment rooms; an open court on the second level is precisely configured to sequester the occupants while maximizing sun exposure throughout the year. The third level provides space for consultation suites and management offices. Five cantilevered bridge-like structures, originating on the third level, offer seating with mountain views. These structures also carry water which falls to pools on the sun deck below. At key afternoon hours the bridges shade portions of the second floor deck. The fluid shape of the roof structure is determined by the relationship of the moving sun to the courtyard. The building form rises to a maximum height on the north side of the court, then begins to drop on the east, still lower on the south and west before rising again on the northwest end.

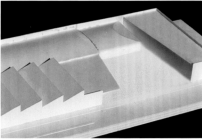

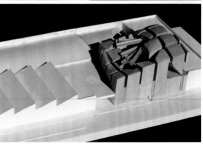

Development sequence: existing, existing removed, proposed Spa

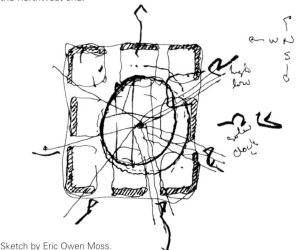

Sketch by Eric Owen Moss.
Light space for Spa

East elevation

Northeast corner

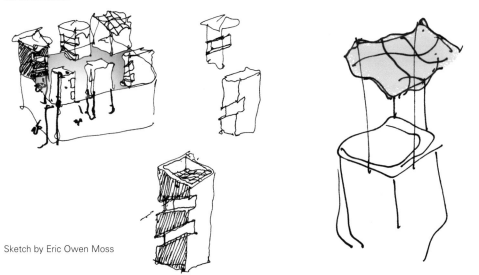

Sketch by Eric Owen Moss

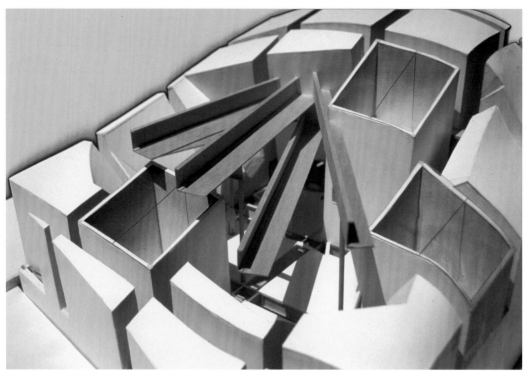

Exterior bridges

Rooftop

Interior perspective

Interior perspective

3505 Hayden Avenue
2003-, Culver City, California

The building design is composed of three major components: the existing building, the courtyard enclosure, and the conference center. The owner requested that the program integrated a variety of meeting spaces with the capability of supporting a wide range of activities for a varying number of individuals. The central courtyard space provides a dynamic and flexible space that can accommodate company-wide meetings and activities. The courtyard enclosure is connected to the conference center that provides a dramatic street elevation. This component of the building houses a large meeting area on the ground level then sub-divides into smaller meeting areas of various sizes above.

The form of the Conference Center is also a response to site constraints. The original cylindrical volume conforms to the height limit and is sloped down toward the North to allow maximum sunlight onto the surrounding plaza. The form is further articulated by the path of the sun, cutting in openings that provide natural light to the meeting rooms within.

The exterior cladding involves the application of strips of expanded metal that provide a substrate for a translucent fiberglass waterproofing. The strips of expanded metal are rolled onto the building and fastened to the CNC milled studs. The design concept is founded upon the idea of "wrapping" the form with continuous bands.

The expanded metal is wrapped counter clockwise around the form and has a tendency to flare upwards as a consequence of the irregular curving shape. The final arrangement of the strips is thus contingent on the curvature of the façade. The roof design that encloses the courtyard is poetically and technically unprecedented: a dense vertical amalgamation of glass and steel rods of varying lengths offers an ever-changing presence of light and sky viewed through a spectacular, Seurat-like field of shining points. The iconic roof is not simply dramatic. In pragmatic terms, the field of rods is both a courtyard enclosing volume, and a versatile, multi-purpose composite that simultaneously provides structural, technical, and staging services for the courtyard.

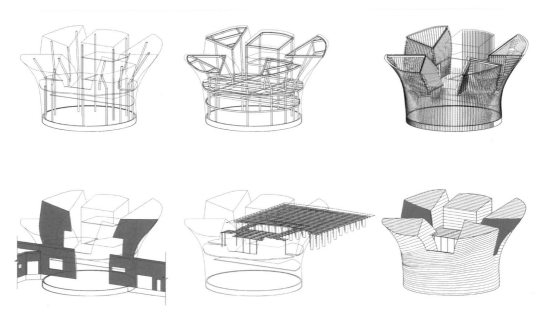

Structural diagram

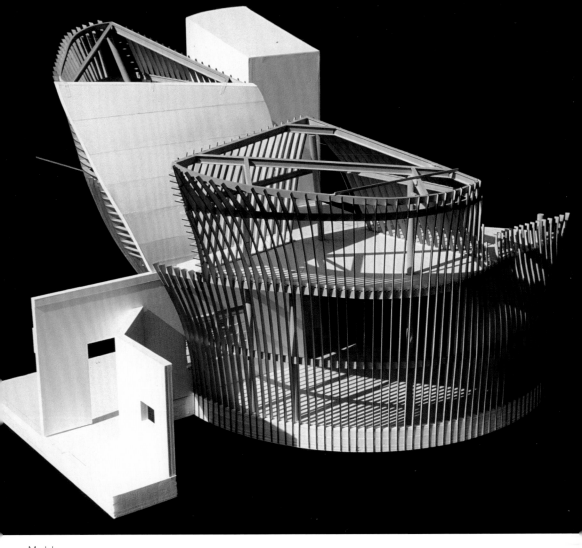

Model

Massing diagram

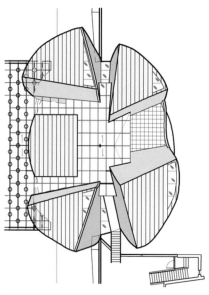

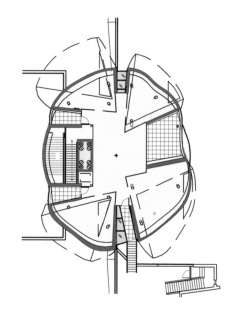

Plans

Northeast perspective,
South elevation, North
elevation and Northwest
perspective

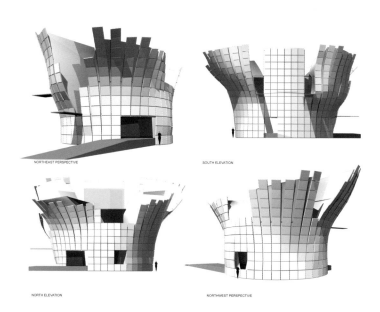

NORTHEAST PERSPECTIVE

SOUTH ELEVATION

NORTH ELEVATION

NORTHWEST PERSPECTIVE

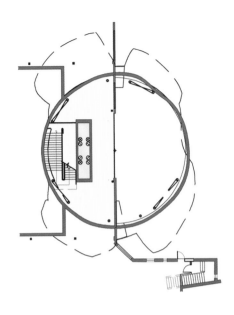
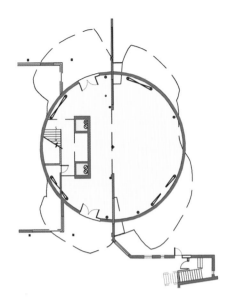

North-South section

West-East section

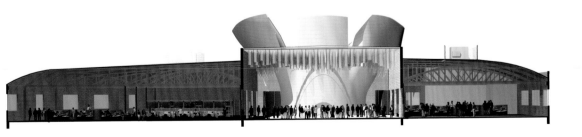

Northeast aerial view; East
elevation

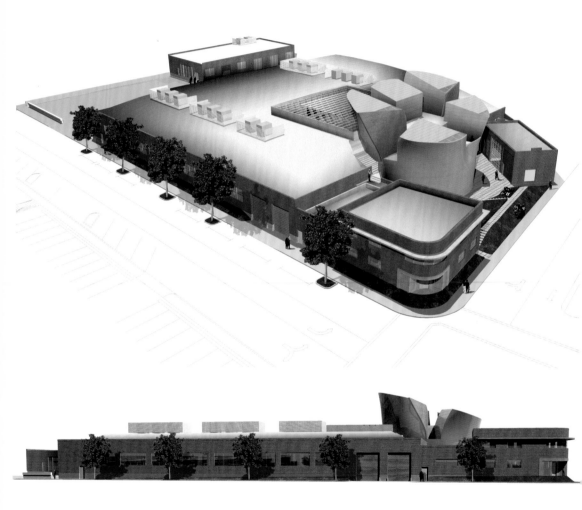

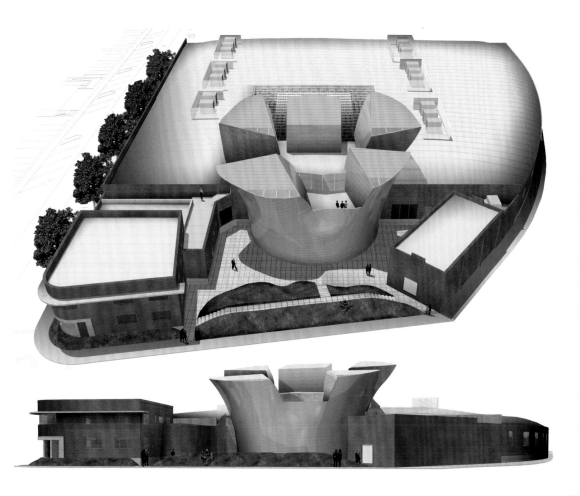

Three Theaters
2003-, Culver City, California

The Conjunctive Points Theater Complex is a mixed-use project that includes three live–action theaters, office and commercial space, restaurants, and a public plaza and park. The 150 feet high building has an area of 335,000 square feet in ten stories and an additional 480,000 square feet in five underground levels of parking.

The building starts as a 100x100 foot square that is extruded across the site from East to West. The resulting volume is then twisted and bent upward on the East side to accommodate an elevated theater-in-the-round with a capacity for 750 fixed seats. On the West side the volume is twisted and pushed downward into the ground to accommodate a raked theater in two

levels that has a capacity for 1,650 spectators, and a multiple use performance space which is located directly above the theater. The shove of the building on the West side creates an indentation in the ground that houses an exterior amphitheater and public garden. The amphitheater can be connected to the adjacent theater to form an interior-exterior theater in the round by removing the wall that divides them.

The central portion, which retains the original 100x100 foot square section of the building, is occupied by commercial space in the lower floors and office space above. The main entrance to the building, located on the South side of the site, is through a large public plaza.

Component diagrams

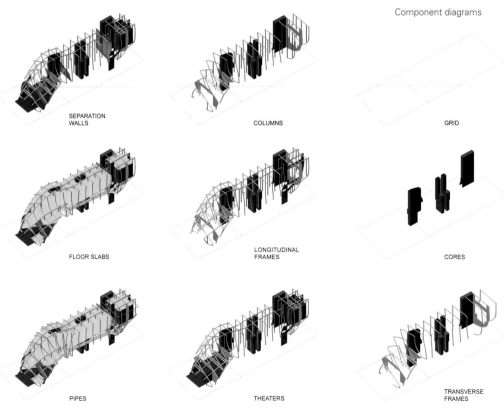

SEPARATION WALLS

COLUMNS

GRID

FLOOR SLABS

LONGITUDINAL FRAMES

CORES

PIPES

THEATERS

TRANSVERSE FRAMES

Aerial South view

Aerial Southeast view

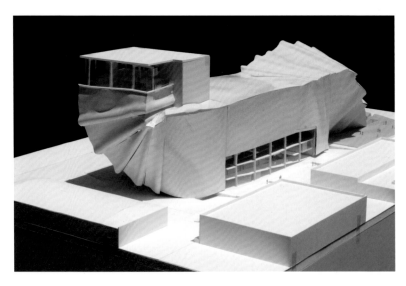

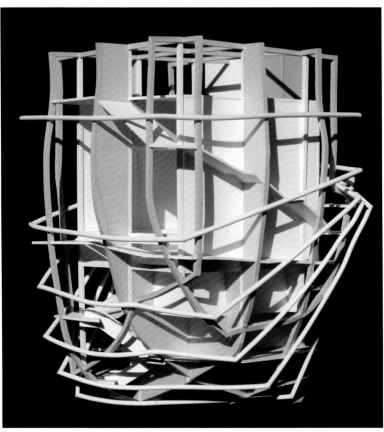

Building Section

Ground floor plan

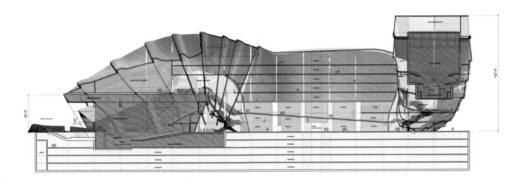

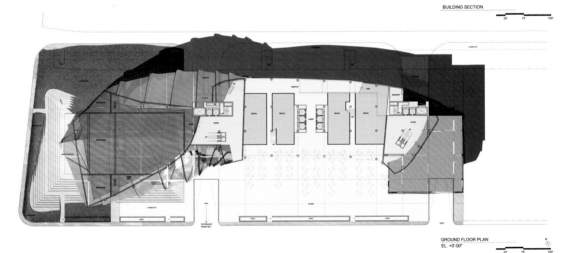

GROUND FLOOR PLAN
EL. +0'-00"

North elevation

East elevation

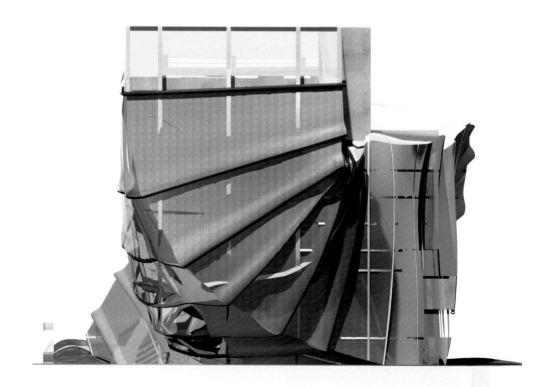

South elevation

West elevation

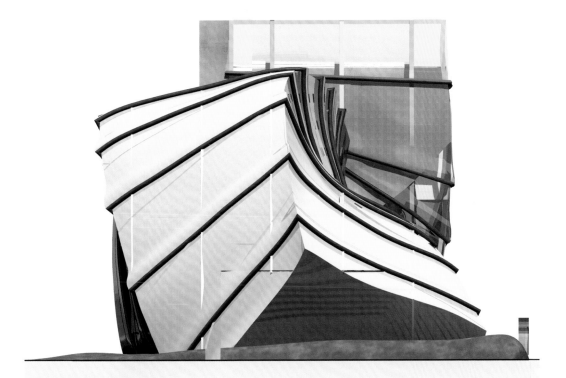

Supper Club
2002-, Culver City, California

A warehouse district transforming into a vital center for creative production is the site for this project. Our client desired a vacant warehouse to be made into a restaurant with multiple functions. Over the course of the day the same dining area and bar should be used in many different ways. The space should be able to accommodate corporate private events, a supper club with dining and live performance or cinema, as well as a dining room that can change size. A space that feels full of activity independent of the number of guests. We imagined three organizational planes dividing the space, which pivot around the existing columns locations. The planes became pivoting walls—spatial dividers. This strategy allows for many different spatial configurations and a flexible use of the space. The existing columns and truss are of wood construction, made for a different purpose. In order to accommodate the mechanical precision required for the operation of these new panels, we replaced them with a new steel truss and columns in the same location. During the day clerestory windows located through the length of the saw-tooth roofs provide the space with ample daylight.

Site plan

The original vacant warehouse

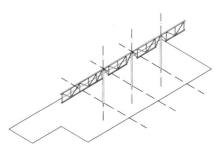

Organizational planes placed perpendicular to truss line, centered about new steel columns. Rotating panels cut when intersecting bar mezzanine volume

New steel truss and columns replace existing wood members in same location.
Planes rotated around structural axis

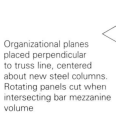
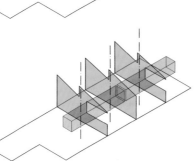
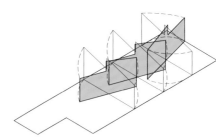

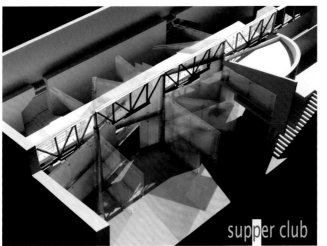

Model

Axonometric

Sketch by Eric Owen Moss

supper club

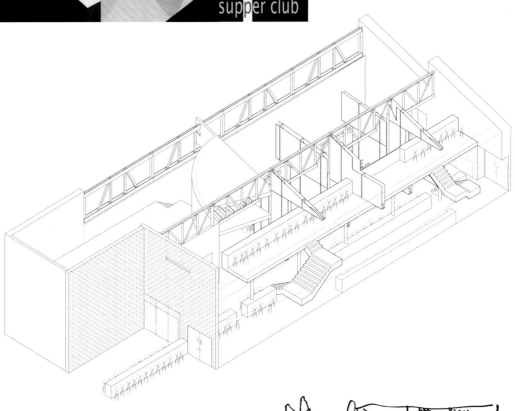

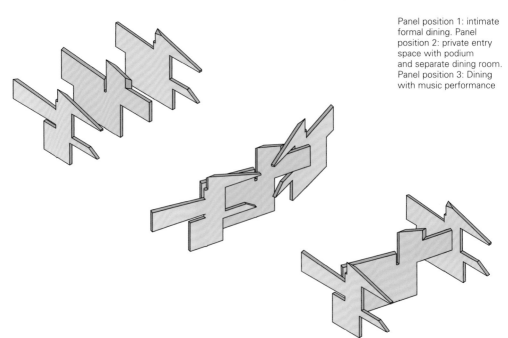

Panel position 1: intimate formal dining. Panel position 2: private entry space with podium and separate dining room. Panel position 3: Dining with music performance

Transverse section

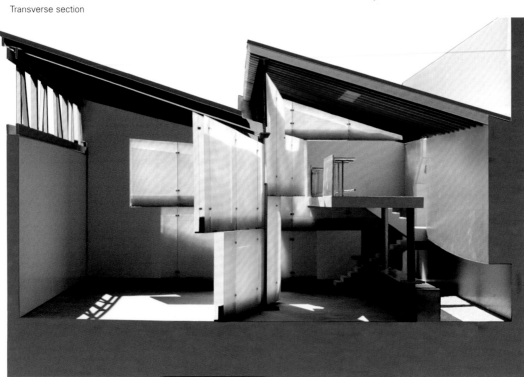

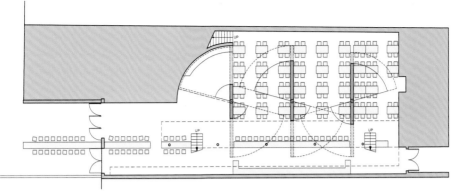

Panel position 1:
intimate formal dining

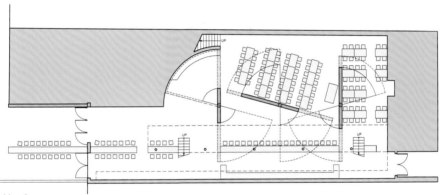

Panel position 2:
private entry space with
podium and separate dining
room

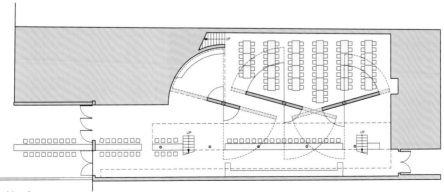

Panel position 3:
Dining with music
performance

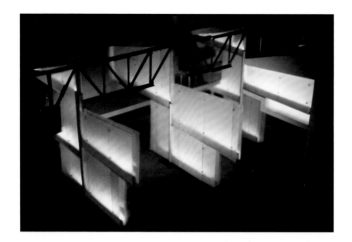

In the evening, the pivoting
glass panels become
sources of illumination

Cinema

Dining and live performance

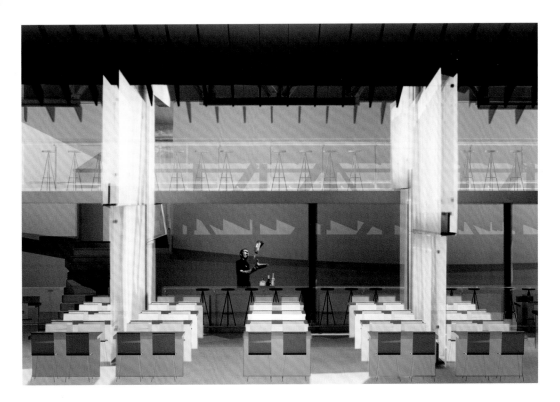

Dining room

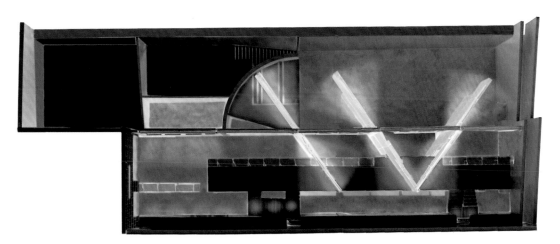

Lighting sheme

Recent Competition Entries

Mariinsky Cultural Center – New Holland
2001-, St. Petersburg, Russia

To the Ice Sculptors

I.

... [to] that which is about to come into being, of the open sea whether or not there is land that lies beyond (Isaiah Berlin, *Russian Thinkers*)

For an American architect it's an astonishing walk along the south bank of the frozen Nieva River in January, 2002... the Winters Palace, the Admiralty, Peter the Great's statue, St. Isaac's Cathedral, New Holland... then south, following the Krukov Canal to the Mariinsky Theatre and St. Nicholas Cathedral. St. Petersburg, Russia's historic "window on the west." But is it still? What's next for the city that began its life as a transformative act of will in a Russian swamp in 1703?

I am an advocate of new architecture. What does that signify for architecture and planning in St. Petersburg? Simply this: history records no permanent solutions. Ideas rise, gain power, dissipate, and are replaced. What remains is the historic record. And that record in St. Petersburg is powerful and compelling. But historic paradigms are provisional. They move. If not in St. Petersburg than elsewhere... but always somewhere and always moving. So why not in St. Petersburg today, propelled by the initial courage of those who founded the city, and the practitioners from east and west who sustained the momentum and implemented the vision?

It's a stunning view from the north bank of the Nieva River. The ice melts and cracks slightly. Perhaps a new conception is about to appear through "the (icy) window on the west".

II.

History would be an excellent thing if only it were true. (Lev Tolstoj)

St. Petersburg is not an assemblage of discrete buildings. Rather it is a chronology of monumental spaces that sweep us along from plaza and canal to building and monument. The center city extends from the Winters Palace on the east to New Holland on the west, then south past the Rimsky-Korsakov Conservatory and the Mariinsky Theatre to St. Nicholas Cathedral.

The center is historically vital because of what it portends. Buildings here originated in different eras and were built in various styles. But the consistent lessons are scale and power. There is no consigning the asymmetry of those public spaces to a sedate conclusion. To architecturally intervene in the area is to exploit its spatial message. The tradition of long diagonal views and expansive public space is open ended. There is room for more. We are encouraged to continue.

III.

... but to give everything its due, two and two make five is also a very fine thing. (Fëdor Dostoevskij, *Notes from Underground*)

The architect has analysed both the New Holland and the New Mariinsky sites not so much as locations for new building "events" in the historic center of St. Petersburg (though they surely suggest that aspect), but rather to understand the two sites as extensions of

Site map

Project site with cultural landmarks shown yellow and religious landmarks shown red.
The instinct to continue the cultural corridor.
To understand the site as an extension of the existing organization of the historic district

the existing organization of the historic district.The New Holland triangle forms the western perimeter of the sequence of public buildings and spaces that runs west along the Nieva River starting at the Winters Palace. The beautiful, old brick warehouses, long used for shipbuilding, define this west edge in a construction language already familiar in the city center. The northeast corner of New Holland should open to pedestrians moving west from Palace Square, or from the subway exit just east of New Holland. These pedestrians will proceed across bridges into New Holland, through a large exhibit hall on the corner and into the open air performance space beyond.

The proposal for New Holland is to sequester the new cultural facilities behind the newly rehabilitated brick structures. The plaza internal to the site has space for 30,000 concert goers; a new outdoor stage and temporary seating for 5000; and a glass enclosed public lobby, lifted above the stage, that contains a 700-seat concert hall. These facilities come into view from inside the brick structures. The brick buildings on the edges of the canals are to be rehabilitated for offices, retail, restaurant, and classrooms and work spaces for the arts. The structures have a double face—open to the canals and city beyond, and to the public plaza where dance, music and impromptu performances will be held.

On the north edge of the New Holland triangle is a new mixed use structure designed to combine hotel rooms, restaurants and an exhibition center that will display inventive technical products from around the world. This exhibit space may be used for a single show, or sub-divided for multiple exhibits and conferences. At the street level are lobbies for both hotel and exhibit center along with the entrance to a new art museum installed in an old boat testing pool below the hotel. The museum will include a collection of experimental contemporary art works. In contrast to the brick of the existing structures, the hotel center is primarily glass with an undulating roof line that offers spectacular views to the city and to the Gulf of Finland.

The center of the New Holland plaza holds a large pool, once used by ship constructors to re-float their boats. That pool will remain in its original shape, connected to the canals that surround the site. Against the north edge of the pool an outdoor stage will be constructed with production and support facilities housed below. Above the water are 5000 temporary theatre seats supported on removable steel structures. And above the stage and seats is the floating glass enclosure—a great spatial promenade in the air, with concourses that lead to the new 700-seat concert hall within. The original structures are brick; the new hotel is glass; and the concert hall combines the two materials.

The east and south elevations of the new hotel and the raised glass promenade and hall are visible from Palace Square to the east and from the Mariinsky to the south, and will punctuate the western skyline of the city. New Holland will not only become an important new cultural destination, but will function as an organizational pivot point, visually uniting eastern and southern portions of the city center through the New Holland apex. The visual exchange between the Mariinsky, the Hermitage, and New Holland establishes three vertices on an east-west/south-north axis, connecting east to south.

Eric Owen Moss

Existing warehouses
rehabilitated and infilled
with new glass volumes

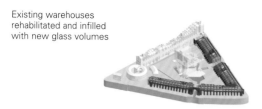

Model

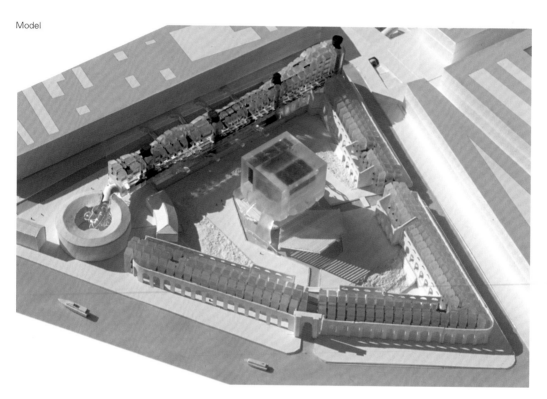

New Holland Hotel-
Conference center-Museum.
The museums. The hotel,
exhibition hall, museum
lobbies, restaurants
and shopping arcade.
The cultural exhibit halls.
The five star skyline hotel

Overall site section:
the rehabilitated warehouse
space, the New Holland
Theater, the terraced public
plaza and the hotel-
conference center-museum

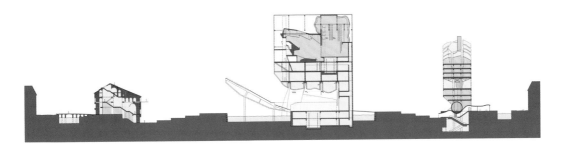

Section through New
Holland Hotel-Conference
center-Museum

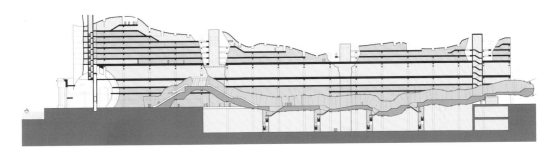

Theater diagrams: plaza
circulation; theater; theater
circulation; plaza and outdoor
stage; support spaces

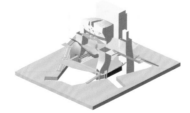

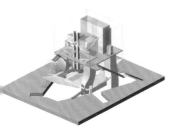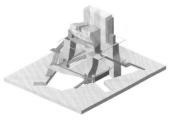

Structural model of the
New Holland Theater

Sketch by Eric Owen
Moss. Initial concept
for New Holland Theater

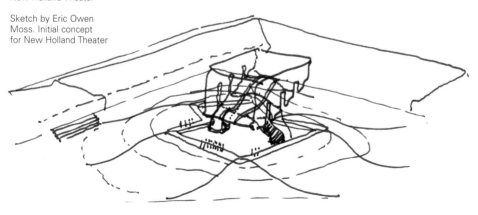

Mariinksy Cultural Center
New Mariinsky Theatre (Version 1)
2001, St. Petersburg, Russia

The project site: (from left to right) Rimsky Korsakov Conservatory, Mariinsky Theater, Krukov Canal, New Mariinsky Theater Site

The New Mariinsky Theatre south of New Holland, seats 2,000 people. A glass bridge is proposed to span the Krukov Canal and join the back stage of the existing theatre with the rear stage production area of the New Mariinsky. The two theatres will share access to sixteen 16m x 16m x 14m stage-house modules. These production units, positioned behind the proscenium tower, will accommodate the most complex assemblies and performance schedules including the staging of four operas simultaneously. Rehearsal halls, design and costume facilities, and administrative offices are also housed in the new structure.

The entry lobby to the new Mariinsky Theatre faces north, with an uninterrupted view to New Holland. A large and gracious entry plaza in the tradition of Palace Square connects the front of the new Mariinsky, the existing Mariinsky, and, by closing the street in front of the Rimsky Korsekov Conservatory, a pedestrian promenade joins all three venues, and opens an important vista south to St. Nicholas Cathedral.

From the public front outside the theatre, the old and New Mariinskys and New Holland's concert hall will be simultaneously in view. Like the New Holland concert hall, the Mariinsky Theatre is enclosed in glass. Three conceptually elastic glass modules or "pillows" are precisely adjusted to form seating, structure, circulation, lobbies, acoustic shell, concourses, and lecture space. Seating in the auditorium is arranged asymmetrically, shaped spatially by extending and adjusting the curved modules which form the building's glass face into the auditorium where the curving material becomes stainless steel.

The Mariinsky ensemble of glass and steel will become one of the world's most technically sophisticated performance venues. With a new New Holland and the New Mariinsky, St. Petersburg, a unique world city with an unmatched cultural pedigree, will launch a new tradition of opera, ballet, music, and architecture far into the next century.

For an American architect, a stroll across the Dvortsovy Bridge over the Nieva River in June, 2005 reveals a surprising reflection in the ice- free water. What an astonishing new skyline shimmering through the "window on the west"...

Eric Owen Moss

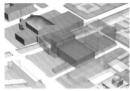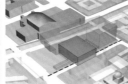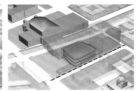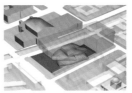

Connection to existing
Mariinsky Theater;
conventional theater
dimensions; compression
by site; extension to public
plazas

Models

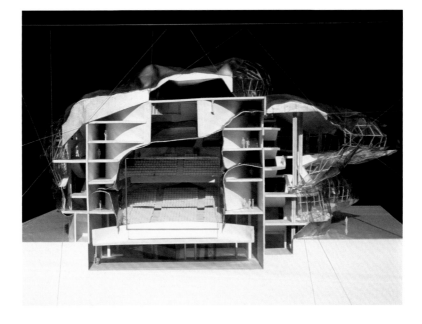

Section AA

Section BB

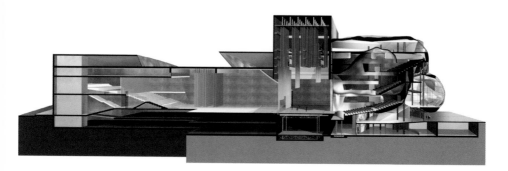

SECTION A-A

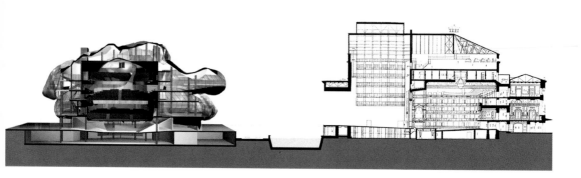

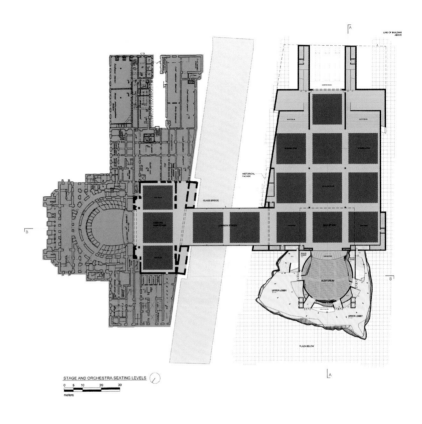

STAGE AND ORCHESTRA SEATING LEVELS

0 5 10   20   30
meters

Theater volume.
Reformation based on
acoustics, seating, and
sight lines

Mariinksy Cultural Center
New Mariinsky Theatre (Version 2)
2001, St. Petersburg, Russia

Perspective from
the Northwest corner

Night perspective

View of the foyer

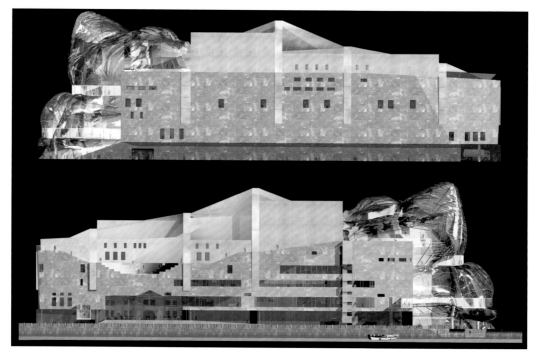

East and West elevations

Longitudinal section

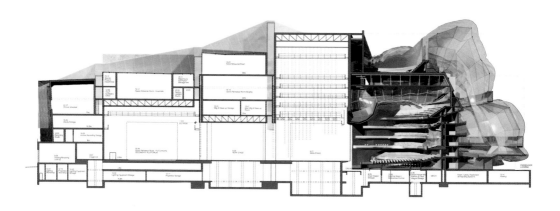

View of house from stage

Orchestra level plan

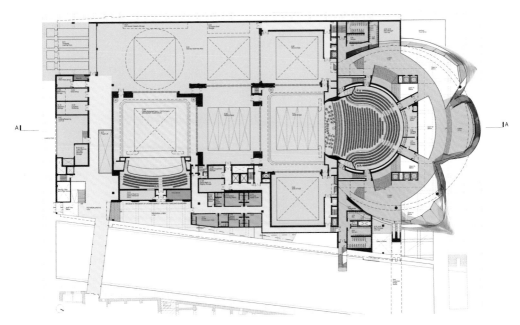

Cairo Museum
2002

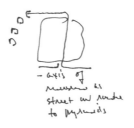

The Grand Egyptian Museum is a unique repository of culture—religious, artistic, linguistic, historic—a 3000 year old ethos which has influenced (and continues to influence) the history which follows.

The durability, the power, the continuing mystery of the Egyptian story—a masterfully controlled definition of a world and its culture—is almost incomprehensible today. How to give this story an architectural form is the question. And the answer requires a re-inventing of the contemporary museum concept.

The proposal here is to present Egyptian culture in myriad ways.

A clear, organizational conception will be legible throughout the project. Multiple spatial configurations, and flexible media venues will facilitate the most complex representation of Egypt's cultural adventure.

The architecture will look to the future, and simultaneously acknowledge the past, in order to communicate the continuing vitality of Egypt's built history. In addition, both the size of the current collection and the definition of Egyptian history will likely change over time. Newspaper headlines regularly confirm spectacular new discoveries and, as a consequence, new theories will be proposed. Egypt's cultural record and its interpretation are subject to revision. The Grand Egyptian Museum will also be a continuous subject for change.

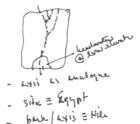

Sketch by Eric Owen Moss

Elevation showing
relationship to Pyramids

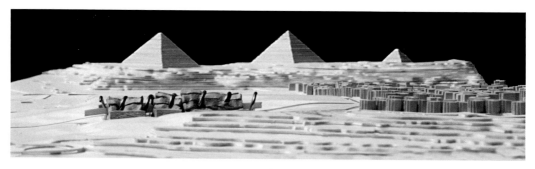

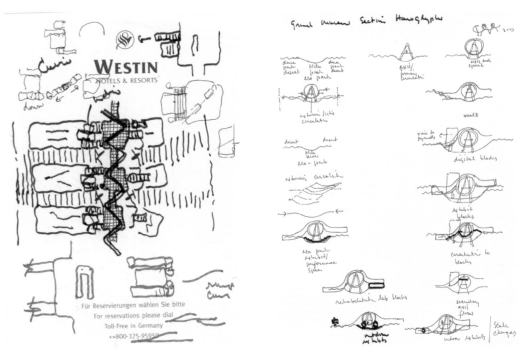

Sketches by Eric Owen Moss

Perspective

PRECEDENT STUDIES

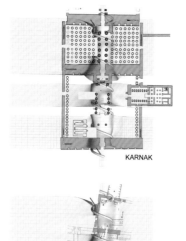

KARNAK

LUXOR

Precedent studies: Karnak
and Luxor

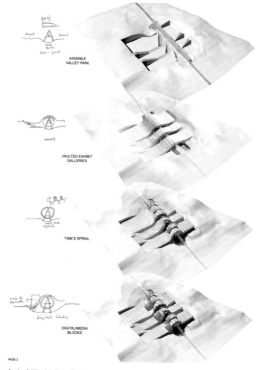

AXIS/NILE
VALLEY PARK

VAULTED EXHIBIT
GALLERIES

TIME'S SPIRAL

DIGITAL/MEDIA
BLOCKS

PAGE 2

Axis-Nile Valley Park;
Vaulted exhibit galleries;
Time's spiral; Digital-media
blocks

Perspective

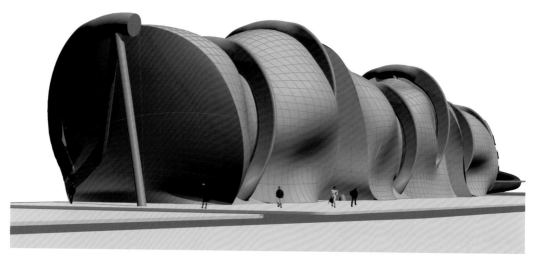

Program organization

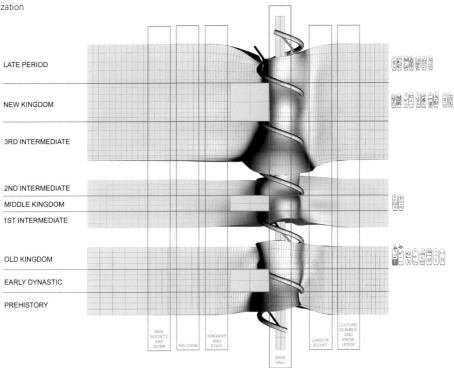

LATE PERIOD

NEW KINGDOM

3RD INTERMEDIATE

2ND INTERMEDIATE

MIDDLE KINGDOM

1ST INTERMEDIATE

OLD KINGDOM

EARLY DYNASTIC

PREHISTORY

MAN, SOCIETY AND WORK   RELIGION   KINGSHIP AND STATE   MAIN HALL   LAND OF EGYPT   CULTURE, SCRIBES, AND KNOW-LEDGE

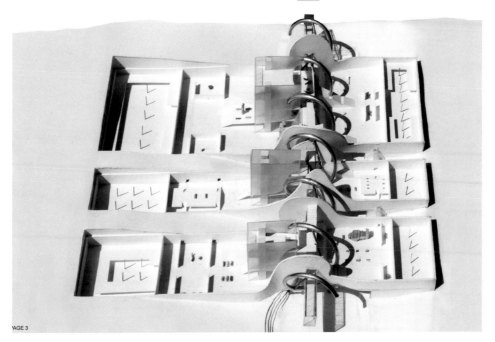

Queen's Museum of Art, Competition Scheme
2003-, Queens, New York

The design strategy for the Queen's Museum of Art un-covers the organizational strengths of the original build-ing and simultaneously suggests new prospects for public participation, exhibition and performance space.

The initial design gesture is surgical: the center portion of the building is removed—roof, perimeter walls, and first and second level circulation, exposing the Panorama[1] enclosure as a primary solid. Steel roof trusses remain and a re-enclosed central volume sur-rounding the Panorama becomes the spatial main event for public promenade, art display, music performance, dramatic presentation, and a multipurpose space for artist expression.

The original floor is removed and the earth exca-vated, leaving a bowl, gently sloping toward a theo-retical center at the base of the Panorama. Temporary seating, oriented toward the Panorama, can be placed within the bowl. Exhibits can be mounted variously over the sloping surface.

Pedestrian circulation on the site has been redi-rected from the Beaux Arts axis, affording the option to pass by the perimeter of the Main Event space, view-ing the exhibits without actually entering the galleries.

The intent of this organizational gesture ("short-cut") is to expose the broader public to contemporary art.

The earth excavated from the bowl will be re-used to form a linear mountain, creating a presence along the Grand Central Parkway. The mountain will become a sculpture garden viewed from the museum, from pass-ing automobiles and most importantly from along a pedestrian walkway.

A laminated glass "drape" re-encloses the Main Event area. The glass will be transparent, translucent, or opaque by turn depending on the exhibits inside. Glass color is controlled by low voltage wires, which alter the glass from clear to opaque milk white.

[1] The *Panorama*, one of the museum's main attractions, is a scale model of the city of New York, most recently re-stored in 1993 by Lester & Associates to bring up to date the streets and buildings cov-ering the considerable sur-face area of the model (867 m², equivalent to 830 km² of the Big Apple).

Aerial view of model

Sketch by Eric Owen Moss

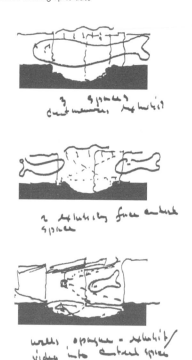

Model of the roof structure

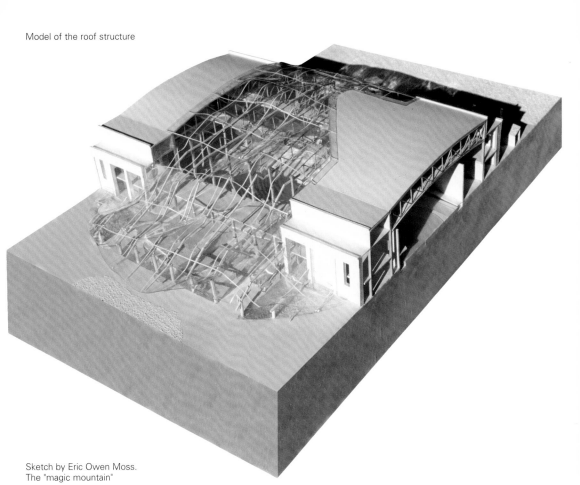

Sketch by Eric Owen Moss.
The "magic mountain"

Sketch by Eric Owen Moss.
The shortcut

Sketch by Eric Owen Moss.
The glass drape

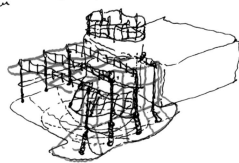

Entry hall

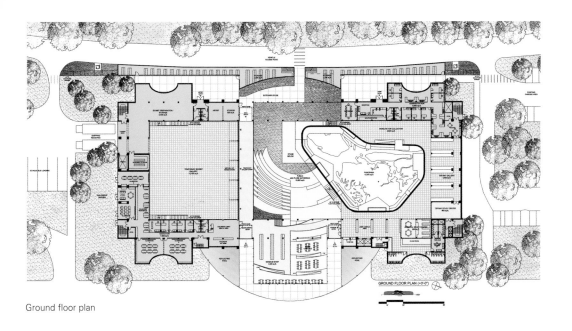

Ground floor plan

Longitudinal section

Elevation

Queen's Museum of Art, Revision
2003-, Queens, New York

East elevation

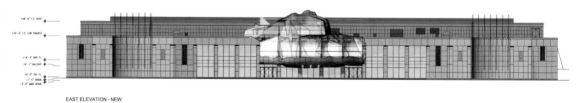

EAST ELEVATION - NEW

EAST ELEVATION - EXISTING

EXISTING STRUCTURE

Diagrams: existing structure; openings made to existing structural slab and walls (mezzanine extension); new steel structure; new faceted glass facade; new curved metal ceiling and roof; new mullion system

Models

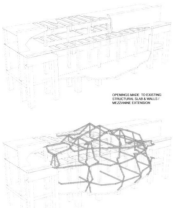

OPENINGS MADE TO EXISTING
STRUCTURAL SLAB & WALLS /
MEZZANINE EXTENSION

NEW STEEL STRUCTURE

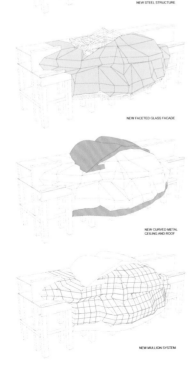

NEW FACETED GLASS FACADE

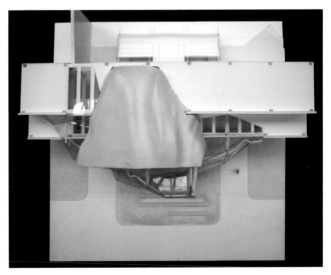

NEW CURVED METAL
CEILING AND ROOF

NEW MULLION SYSTEM

Montreal Theatre Offices
2003, Montreal, Canada

SITE ORGANIZATION

The Balmoral Block in Montreal is both an urban planning and a civic architecture subject. The new plan for the Balmoral site should utilize planning and architectural means to promote a more extroverted sensibility as the public moves across the city and experiences the prospect of connectivity rather than a separation of blocks and events.

The project must embody a civic presence comparable with Montreal's contemporary civic and business structures. The building is conceived as an entity, a single clear and powerful voice for Montreal, the Quebec government and the world of music performance.

A fundamental design decision was to lift the concert hall to a 30-meter height above the street. Theatre access is by elevator, and most importantly by the north/south public walkway gallery which turns vertically near Maisonneuve Boulevard and becomes an enclosed vertical street of escalators and decks. The vertical walk contains the north/south gallery, emphasizing the visibility of public movement along this vertical promenade to the concert hall. From the stack of escalators and decks, spectacular views are available to the old city to the north, to the new city east and west, and to the St. Laurence River to the south.

A number of the program components are visible in the design of the building elevations. Each element has an identifiable configuration on the façade. The administrative offices are legible on the west elevation as a curving glass façade. The curve is determined by the movement of the sun, and the glass components will be repetitive modules positioned variously to mitigate the effect of direct sunlight on the perimeter glazing. The concert hall and support facilities are brick construction (reminiscent of the old city) behind a smooth, transparent glass façade on both east and west elevations.

The proposed new project is less object, less wall, less city divider, and more an aperture, a design and site planning model for re-uniting disparate portions of the downtown area within a building that re-interprets the components of the historic city to create a contemporary vision which includes the old in the new.

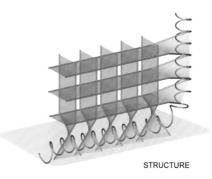

STRUCTURE

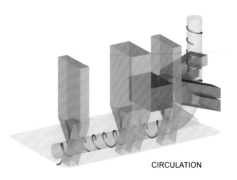

CIRCULATION

Site organization: structure; circulation; program distribution

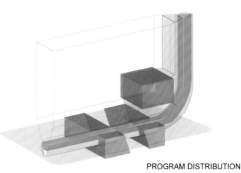

PROGRAM DISTRIBUTION

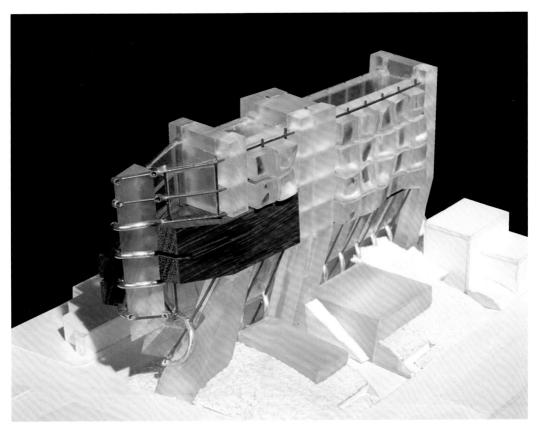

Study model

Plan

Aerial Montage

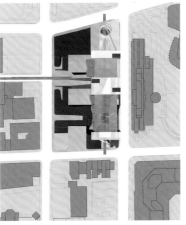

José Vasconcelos Library of Mexico
2003, Mexico City, Mexico

The National Library of Mexico City is not simply a significant addition to the city center. Uniquely, the project carries with it the aspirations of Mexico's government for an informed, literate, and productive citizenry.

A literate citizenry elevates and enlivens the culture, generates ideas that propel the economy, and vigorously engages the on-going discourse on national and world affairs. A productive contemporary population is a literate population, one which must have access to the information and ideas that will re-constitute Mexico's future.

The library is more than books and digital information. The library is a microcosm of the city. The library is the center that will sustain and advance the lives of Mexico's citizens and provide the tools that will allow those citizens to continually renew the culture of Mexico and to exchange ideas and information world wide. The National Library will symbolize the achievements of Mexico's past, affirm the vast potential of its present, and most imaginatively, offer the tools to a most productive future to the people of Mexico.

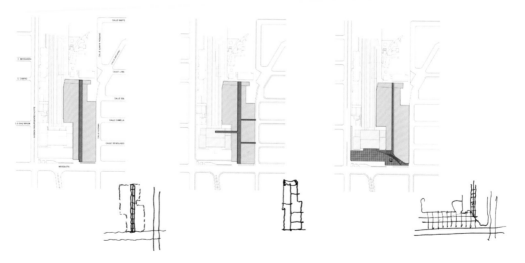

Avenida de los Libros.
Creation of major
pedestrian avenue through
library site. Library as
extension of the city

Surrounding streets.
Extension of Mexico City
street grid into library

Plaza de Libros
y Ferrocarrilles.
Library and train station
share the plaza

Canyons of the sun.
Each court has a specific
function associated with
the functions of the library

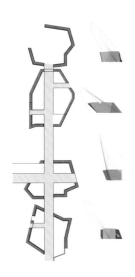

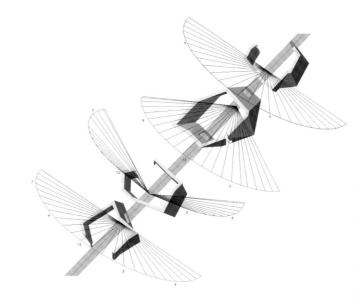

Model

Model photo

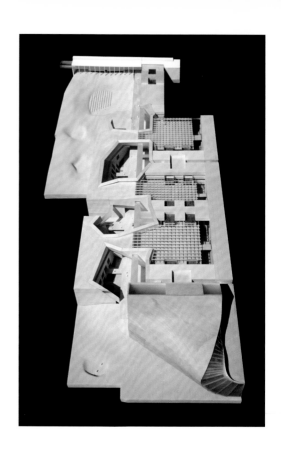

Lobby section

Elevations

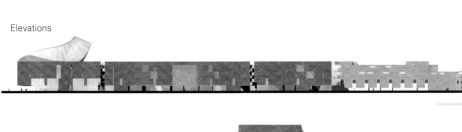

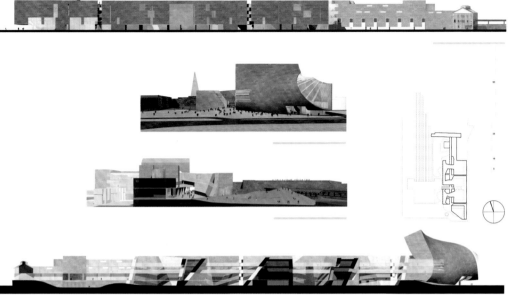

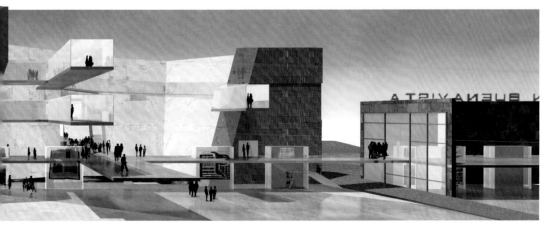

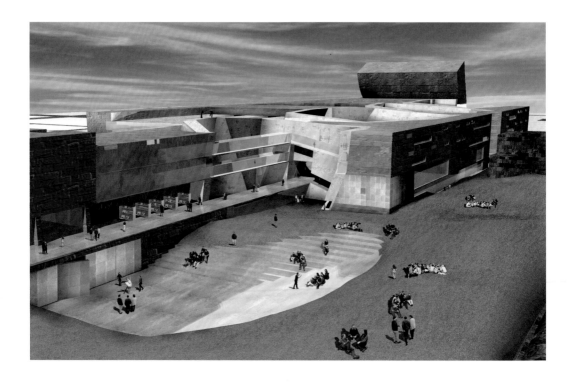

Public circulation through
library. +4 m level

Public circulation through
library. +9 e +14 m

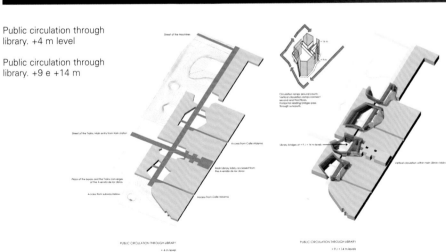

Smithsonian Institution
2003, Washington D.C.

The design solution for the enclosure of the Patent Office Building courtyard offers a remarkable opportunity to re-confirm the building's unique institutional and architectural pedigree—"America's temple to the industrial arts"—by adding a dramatic contemporary chapter to the building's history. Fortuitously, the buildings' original purpose—the display of inventor's models submitted with patent applications—embodies a spirit of technical and artistic progress that the existing building will share with the newly enclosed courtyard.

The roof design that encloses the courtyard is poetically and technically unprecedented: a dense vertical amalgamation of glass and steel rods of varying lengths offers an ever-changing presence of light and sky viewed through a spectacular, Seurat-like field of shining points. Simultaneously, the composite structure reaffirms the prominence of the original courtyard experience—the granite and sandstone walls that form the "great room", now sharpened and re-focused in a new, reflected light. The iconic roof is not simply dramatic. In pragmatic terms, the field of rods is both a courtyard enclosing volume, and a versatile, multi-purpose composite that simultaneously provides structural, technical, and staging for the great room.

Sketch by Eric Owen Moss.
Possible configurations
of the courtyard:
performance; exhibit; forest
of rods; sculpture garden;
water; lecture

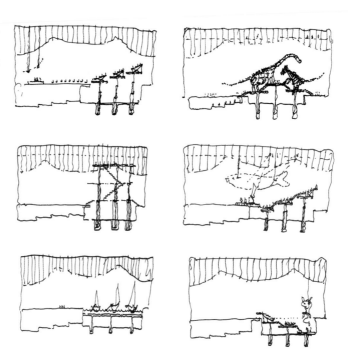

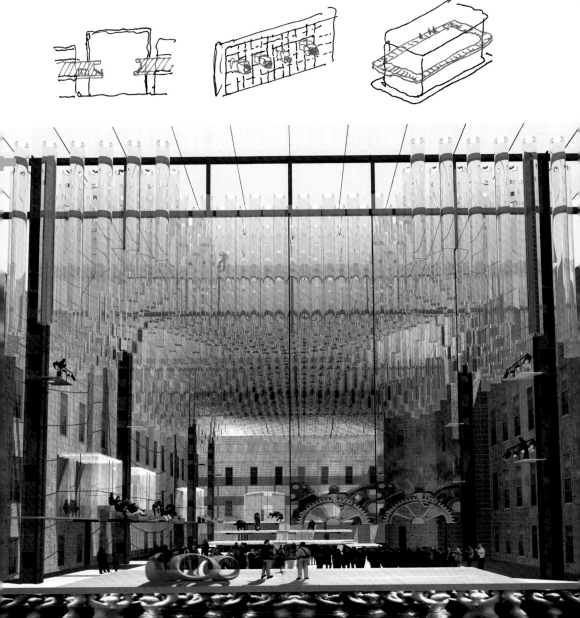

Sketch by Eric Owen
Moss. Gallery extension
diagram

Central space

Longitudinal section

Structural components:
base structure; glass box
enclosure; steel cables;
glass rods

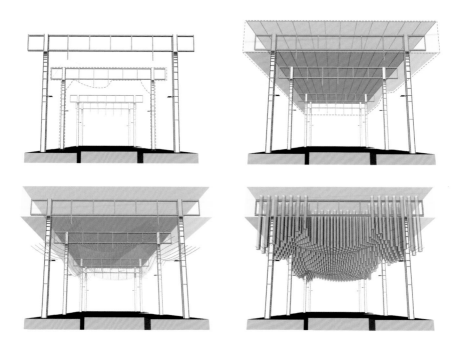

Section model

Courtyard floor plan

Second floor plan

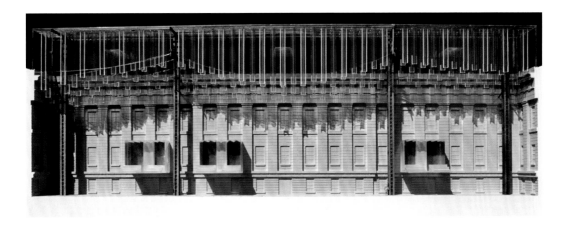

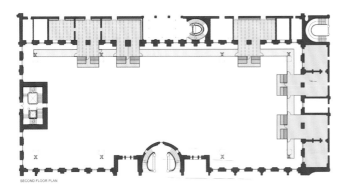

SECOND FLOOR PLAN

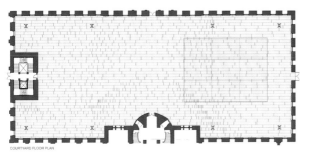

COURTYARD FLOOR PLAN

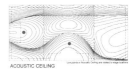

ACOUSTIC CEILING   Low plants in Acoustic Ceiling are related to stage locations

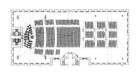

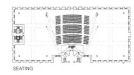

SEATING

Acoustic diagrams

Guangzhou Museum
2004, Guangzhou, Cina

The city of Guangzhou is growing at an unprecedented rate, particularly in a southern direction toward the Pearl River. The site area of the new Guangdong Museum and Opera House offers a unique planning opportunity to resolve this rapid urban growth where the expanding city meets the Pearl River, and to provide residents and visitors to the city with a new and unprecedented experience of art and culture.

We propose two conceptual design metaphors for the planning of the museum site: first, the Mountain with 4 Peaks and second, the Glass Forest. These two new organizational ideas will resolve the intersection of the expanding city, the Culture and Art Square, the Museum site, and the River, offering the citizens of Guangdong province a powerful and compelling sequence of spaces for promenading, exhibition, performance, and landscape in the intermediate zone where the city ends and the river begins.

The Mountain with 4 Peaks will alter an essentially flat landscape by introducing a new land form or promontory which rises from four points out of the horizontal museum site. As the land form grows, it extends west, connecting with the raised land form of the new Opera House. In a sense, the newly elevated ground separates the city from the river, and creates a raised platform of land from which to view north to the City, south to the River, east to the Museum, or west to the Opera House.

This conceptual landform—the Mountain with 4 Peaks—is generated by the 4 primary organizational gallery components in the museum program: Art, History, Nature, and Temporary. These 4 elements will become the 4 Glass Gallery Cubes or towers, each 45m x 45m x 45m, which contain the major exhibition and support spaces for each of the museum departments.

Running east and west along the top of the new ridge is the Long Art March, a linear pedestrian path 7 meters wide that connects the Culture and Art Square with the new Museum and the Opera House. This new walk will become the primary pedestrian route to the new museum. Paralleling the 'Art' March is the new Glass Forest, a dense grouping of transparent hollow glass tubes—Glass Trees—that are aligned precisely on either edge of the pedestrian walk. The Glass Trees will be 7 meters high and 0.75 meters in diameter, measured from the surface of the re-configured earth. As the terrain varies in height the glass cylinders will telegraph the new profile of the land. In addition, the tubes will bend in the wind and echo the wind's sounds.

The Long 'Art' March and Glass Forest conclude in an open area at the center of the 4 glass towers in a large contemplation and seating space that surrounds the walk and the museum entrance. This is a sequestered, introverted space, enclosed by the 4 Glass Gallery Cubes and the Glass Forest, with concrete seats on a descending glass cavity, but open to the sky. Performances and exhibits here are also possible.

The Central Hall on the main floor is a flexible, multi-purpose area where huge, temporary exhibitions will be installed, or large audiences assembled in temporary bleachers for dance, music or dramatic performances. From the primary exhibition floor one looks up and out through the central glazed area, past the seats in the contemplation space above to the 4 Glass Gallery Cubes and Glass Forest beyond. The Glass Forest tubes provide shafts of directed natural light to the main space where possible. Additionally, the Glass Trees, lit electrically, will provide directed light to the exhibits on the floor below and light the night sky and the glass walls of the 4 Glass Gallery Cubes.

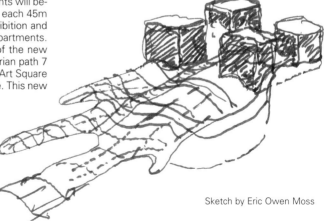

Sketch by Eric Owen Moss

Context model

The Glass Forest

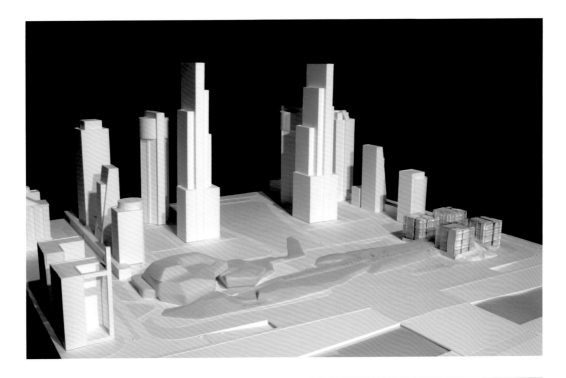

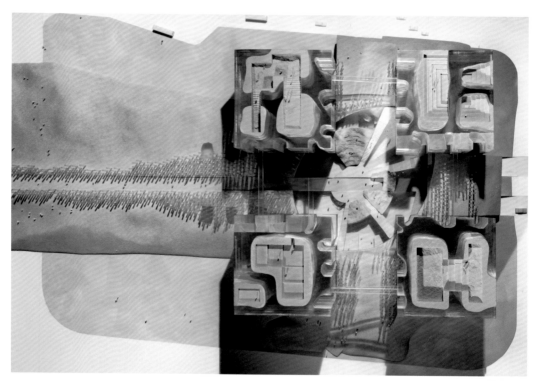

Model site plan

Transverse and longitudinal
section

View along the Long Art
March

Following pages:
Central lobby perspective

Robbins School
2004, Trenton, New Jersey

The design strategy for the Robbins School uncovers the organizational strengths of the original building and simultaneously suggests new prospects for community involvement, and an academically challenging environment.

The Instructional Commons will become a symbol of the Robbins School and its Community—Faculty, Children, and Neighborhood. The "event" space, with a large open floor and movable bleacher seating, facilitates both formal and happenstance events of every sort. The Main Event area is surrounded by a number of ancillary "resource" spaces which can be used individually or as support areas for presentations in the larger space.

The "All-Purpose Court" creates a sky lit shared interior space usable by the surrounding classes, for formal and informal assemblies, for exhibits, neighborhood gatherings, and for impromptu events and play. The court can be opened to the air by retracting the glass enclosure below the balcony. Roll-down projection screens extend from the Main Event above as needed.

The "Transition Floor' is the zone of transition between the original structure and the proposed new construction. The "T" Floor joins components of historic and new architecture and will hold the shared program spaces in the project. The Main Event / Instructional Commons, Art and Music Rooms, Cafeteria, and Computer Labs will be located at this "vertical" center of the building, equidistant and equally accessible from the floors above and the floors below.

New Classroom / Resource Centers are located above the existing building. "Sky boxes" on the roof add outdoor play space with sod roofs, photovoltaic systems, and the city all in view. Pre-Kindergarten and Kindergarten classrooms are added at grade with a sequestered outdoor play area for the youngest children.

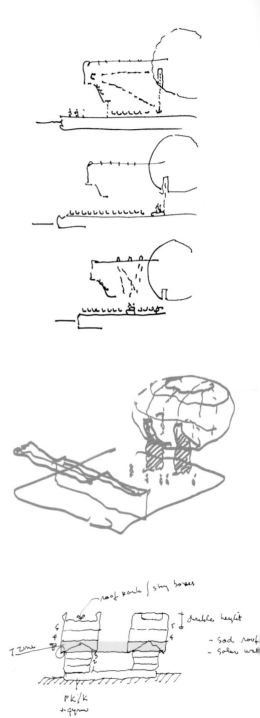

Sketch by Eric Owen Moss. Indoor performance. Outdoor play. Indoor-outdoor. "The Great Hall". Central stage. Indoor-outdoor performances

Sketches by Eric Owen Moss

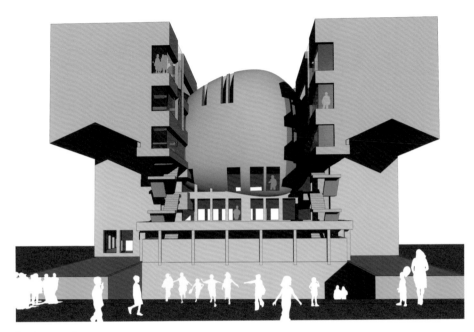

Front perspective

Perspective from
playground

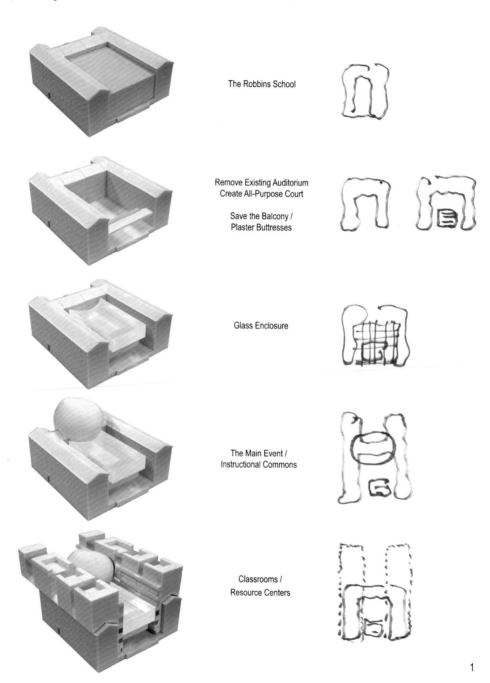

The Robbins School

Remove Existing Auditorium
Create All-Purpose Court

Save the Balcony /
Plaster Buttresses

Glass Enclosure

The Main Event /
Instructional Commons

Classrooms /
Resource Centers

1

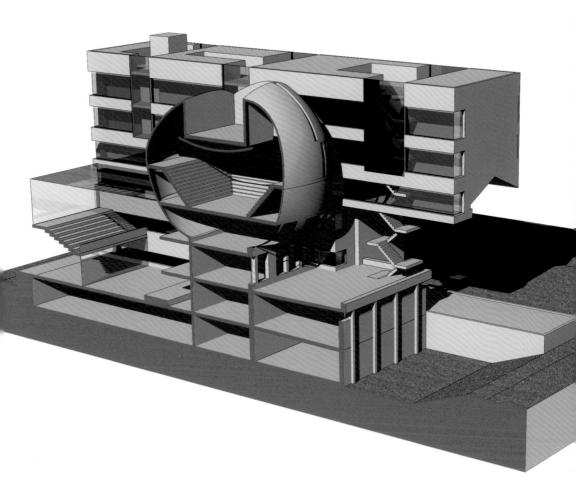

Other Works

708 House
1979-1982, Los Angeles, California

This house was originally built in the tradition of the Los Angeles Case Study Houses[1], but it would probably be more accurate to call it a second-hand Case Study House. It's straightforward: clean, orderly, regular, sparse, white (all of the words that you could get out of Hitchcock and Johnson's International Style).

Over a number of years there had been a whole series of additions proposed, not done, and revised. This one, which was finally done in the early 1980s, was a practical accommodation; it just added some aspects to the program that were needed in order to make the building livable, in an ordinary sense. But it also represented an investigation, not so much into an order of space or volume, but into a series of pieces, or the making of pieces, and the making of surfaces, which then evolved or was developed in other projects.

The 708 House was the first case where a second floor was built over a first floor without removing the first floor roof structure. That process is revealed in a zone at the front of the building (between old roof and new floor) which became a tile stripe.

Street elevation

Window detail

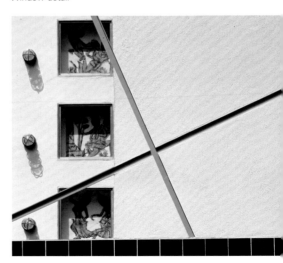

[1] The Case Study House Program was promoted between 1945 and 1960 by John Entenza, director of the "Arts & Architecture" magazine, an idealist and intelligent supporter of modern architecture. His programme enabled young modernists to conduct broad-ranging experiments on ideal homes in Los Angeles—the detached family home—which, by promoting the construction of small, low-cost modular homes, anticipated the building boom that took place at the end of the Second World War to make up for the shortfall in housing. Thanks to the support of "Arts & Architecture", which was read and highly considered throughout the world, the Case Study House Program represented the moment of greatest influence of the International Style in the Los Angeles area. Through buildings of an extraordinary creativity, it bore witness to the interesting research and experimentation, the high architectural level attained here and hitherto only appreciated in the circumscribed circles of the intellectual élite.

Rooftop terrace

Corner detail

Petal House
1982-1984, Los Angeles, California

The original building, which was about 1100 square feet, required a number of programmatic additions and extensions. In order to enlarge the living room on the south side of the entrance, it was pulled out, and then a porch was tacked on to the face of it. As you walk in the entrance, you're walking a line which gives you bilateral symmetry on the first floor. The guest room, on one side of the line, and the porch, on the other, are identical in roof form and in outline, but one is a solid and one is a void. The void is a cage, which is the first time that the re-bar railing is used. The window in the porch wall is the analog of the one in the living room wall. So it is symmetrical and balance on the first floor, except that it isn't, because one form is solid and the other is the inverse.

The building is higher, significantly (by one floor), than all of the other buildings in the area. So it distinguishes itself in that way, and also it has an association with the Santa Monica Freeway, which happens to run right by it. The way the petals are set up, you can hide behind them, and be unseen, or you can go to the corners and look out.

Front entry

View from pool

View from freeway

View from pool

Lindblade Tower
1987-1989, Culver City, California

The Lindblade Tower building is first about the tower itself. The roof has an orientation to the corner and to the freeway beyond. The masonry walls and piers have an orientation to the street system. The roof, which is pyramidal, is turned; but it's cut off on the orthogonal walls. The skewed pyramid would have extended over the square of the walls, but the extension is cut off, except on the front.

There's a plaster wall that runs through the tower, intersects it, and separates inside from outside. When you're on the east side of that wall, you're inside; when you're on the west side of that wall, you're out-side. There's a system of masonry which is columns and walls, which acknowledges the streets and repeats its orthogonal geometries. Then the roof has a different geometry; it's now two buildings becoming one, and not becoming one. And the third piece, the plaster wall, is doing a little bit of both and neither. It has a geometry that is not aligned with the street. That is because we retained the original shed roof and the original trusses, which were supported on plaster walls. We had to save the trusses because we told the city that the project was a remodel. So the plaster walls remained as well.

Street elevation

Interior garden

Conference room

Paramount Laundry
1987-1989, Culver City, California

There is a bridge in the building that connects two new pieces of floor. That bridge is held up by vitrified clay column legs that hold up glue-lam beams, which hold up the fins, which hold up the roof of the vault. The glue-lams also hold wooden T's, which hold smaller beams, which hold the walkway that runs from one end of the third floor to the other. The area under that walkway was always thought of as a sort of stage, so the central column on the south span has been removed, allowing the glue-lam beam and the two remaining legs to act as a proscenium arch. The insertion of the bridge into the building happened to conflict with an existing wooden truss. So a portion of that truss was removed, and steel—a steel tube, a steel pipe, a steel channel— was inserted as surgical replacement of the amputated truss so that the bridge could go through.

Street elevation

Colonnade

Structural detail

Interior workspace

Gary Group
1988-1990, Culver City, California

The new building provides management offices and design space for an entertainment/marketing firm. The project was conceived as a picaresque novel with a series of discontinuous adventures involving the same participants; the novel can be opened at any point and read either forward or backward.

The building has two entrances. The first, facing the street to the north, is cut into a nearly free-standing concrete block wall which inclines leeward and rests on steel ribs implanted in the adjacent wall. A clock, attached to the west end, faces the parking lot. The second entrance, cut through a wall embellished with chains, wires, pipes, and re-bar, opens directly west.

Inside is a group of workstations arranged within a cruciform plan/gable section. Workstations mix with four small, austerely landscaped courtyards. At the center is a pool, open to the sky, with steel showerheads that drop water through a marble chute into the pool. Adjoining the "crucigable" area is a corridor terminated by a private conference room. A conical steel cap supported on wood and steel legs punctures the half-pyramid skylight roofing the room. South of the corridor is a two-story area for both private offices and open counter for graphic artists. The vaulted roof, supported by two bowstring trusses, is interrupted by two enormous aluminum, glass, and sheet metal funnels that deposit natural light inside.

Front elevation

The conference room

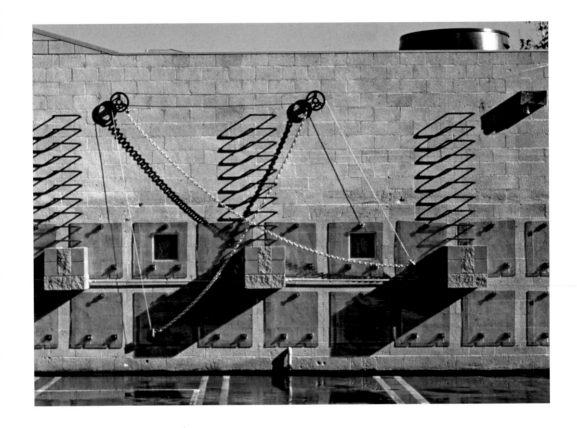

8522 National Boulevard Complex
1986-1990, Culver City, California

On National Boulevard, a main thoroughfare in Culver City, five warehouses adjoin one another, forming a single building. The buildings, constructed between the 1920s and 40s, are all long span spaces with clerestory windows facing either east or north. There was never any design attempt to coordinate an earlier building with a later one. By 1986, the building—used as a plastics factory—was filled with partitions, hung ceilings, ducts, sprinkler lines, and rooms of every size.

The exterior was dilapidated. The owner decided to have the building reconstituted and make it available for commercial use. A steel canopy was stretched across the street elevation, propped on struts extended from the existing wall. An elliptical entry court was cut into the original building, exposing a piece of truss structure to the street. The wall of the ellipse was constructed of concrete block and both truss and ellipse were partially covered with steel.

A pedestrian entry ramp from the street leads into the court then through the entry door to a causeway organized around an existing column system. The hallway consists of three pieces: a frame wall (painted drywall,) an arch wall (speckled blue plaster,) and a glass wall, which occurs occasionally.

The causeway leads to a middle lobby, newly skylit, with a perimeter wall of block and plaster, related in plan form to the entry ellipse. Turning south, there is a second causeway which leads to a large meeting room.

A third ellipse (inclined in section) has been built into an existing room with walls of concrete block. The new meeting room walls are birch plywood, attached to the studs with brass screws. Studs are partially exposed to reveal the mechanism by which the room was constructed.

Entry court

The conference room

View over office space

Stair to second floor
conference room

Skylight set into existing
fabric

Gasometer D-1
1995-1996, Vienna, Austria

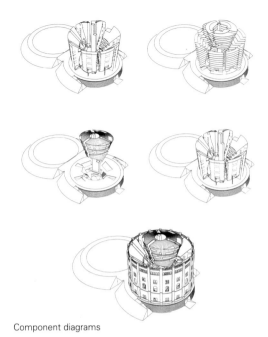

On the outskirts of Vienna, adjacent to the Autobahn, are four cylindrical masonry tanks, 60 meters in diameter and 65 meters high. The tanks, each with a steel and wood domed roof, were built at the end of the nineteenth century to hold natural gas that was piped to Vienna.

Because of their historic role in the city, the exterior facades of the tanks must be preserved. Mr. Gunther Bishoff, the client, asked four architects to study the implications of locating 15,000 square meters of public housing along with retail, commercial, entertainment, and parking facilities within the tank. Although the facades could not be disturbed, it was possible to alter the profile of the domed roof.

The key to the solution was to divide the housing blocks into triangular wedges with light wells in between. The housing code of Vienna has strict recommendations for the provision of natural light in all living areas, and the wedge plan facilitates the entry of light to interior rooms. At the base of the tank is a public space called the "pentasphere", which holds retail, commercial, entertainment and parking.

Component diagrams

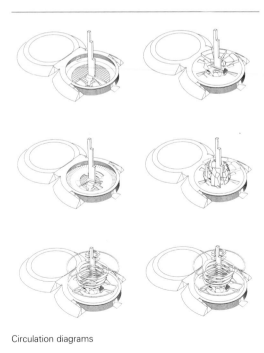

Circulation diagrams

Following pages:
Models

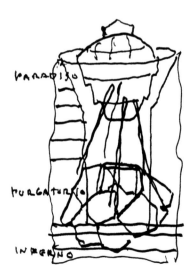

Sketch by Eric Owen Moss

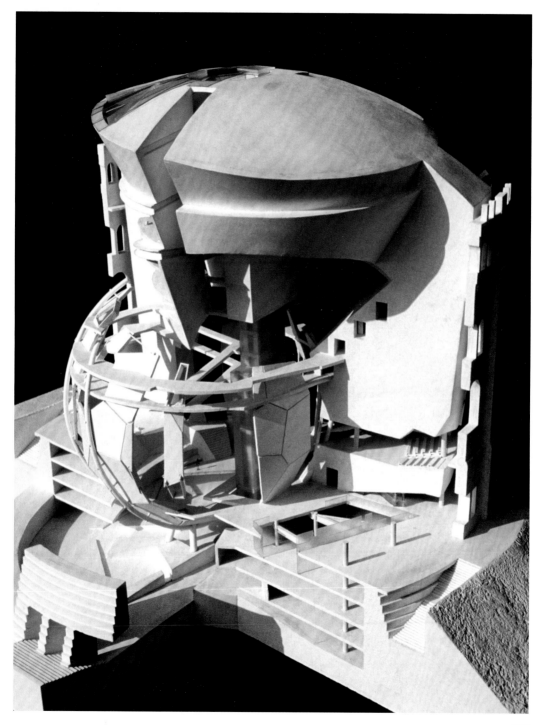

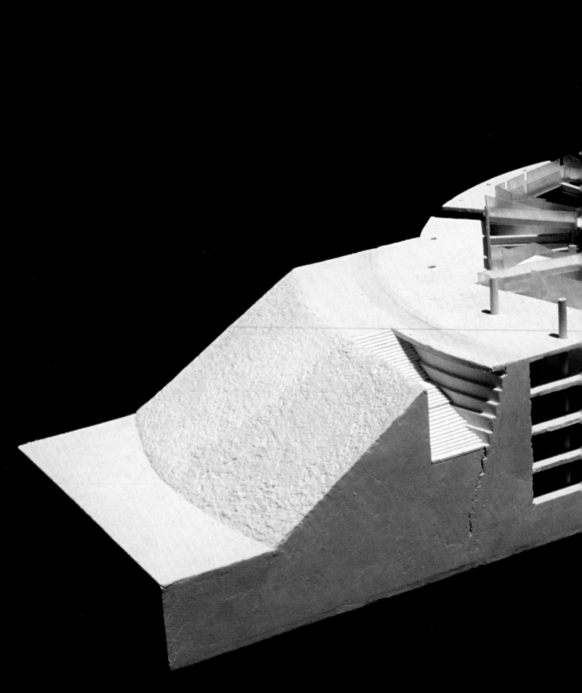

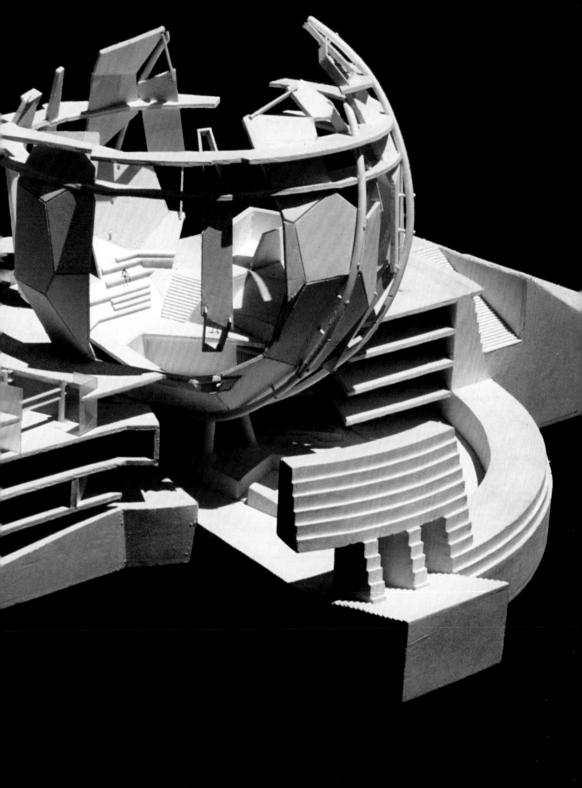

Franklin Tower
2004-, Los Angeles, California

The Franklin Tower project is an ongoing conceptual study for the development of a high-rise residential tower, combined with street oriented retail amenities, a storage warehouse block, and requisite parking. Located in the heart of historic Hollywood, just one block north of the storied intersection of Hollywood and Vine and across from the iconic Capital Records building, the proposed tower is intended to signal the ongoing revitalization of a once thriving community center and major tourist destination.

The project is organized into three distinct programmatic elements that are linked together within one sculptural building envelope. The building is anchored by the warehouse block that occupies three floors along the west boundary of the site. To the east, a retail block originating along Vine Street, twists and extends upward, culminating in a glass-faced residential tower. The twist allows a reorientation of the housing units in order to maximize views of the local Hollywood Hills. A rooftop pool and large billboard sign cap the top of the structure, taking advantage of local zoning ordinances designed to promote the idea of building as advertisement.

The resultant building form is offered as a visual reciprocity with the adjacent Capital Records building. Both independent, both original, both of similar scale, the old will be reflected in the new. Together, the two structures will provide a gateway into a new Hollywood.

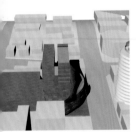

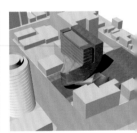

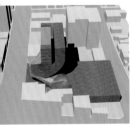
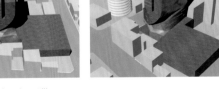
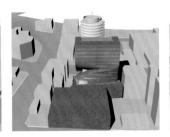
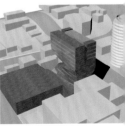

Animation stills

South elevation

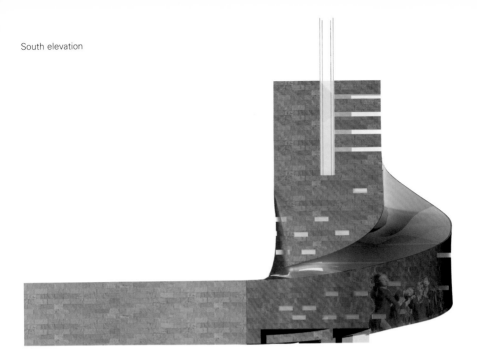

East elevation

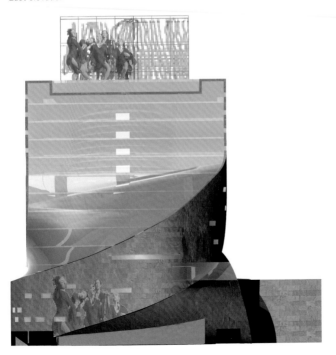

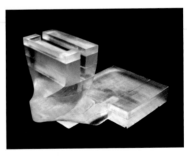

Concept model

North elevation

West elevation

The Freight Yard
2004-, Los Angeles, California

The project began as a hypothesis for a new mixed-use development on four contiguous parcels adjacent an existing 1909 historic reinforced concrete freight depot currently housing the Southern California Institute of Architecture. In 2000, SCI-Arc was invited by the City of Los Angeles to move from the suburbs into the freight depot on the eastern edge of downtown in the hopes of creating a galvanizing engine for the redevelopment of the area.

Unlike other large-scale developments in Los Angeles in recent years, the proposed project has no inherent programmatic meaning such as the new Cathedral or the Music Center. It must derive meaning and program from the disparate communities that surround it, and reconcile the interests of developers, politicians, and community members with those of the students and faculty of SCI-Arc. The result is part community center with public parks, walkways, restaurants, and galleries, part market rate high-rise residential, and part retail. The residential component proposes 1200 market-rate units, 100 units dedicated to SCI-Arc students, and 50 affordable units for the neighborhood community. The retail component wraps the street frontage on three sides. The extension of Traction Avenue through the site interrupts this component providing a public connection from the site perimeter into a large central plaza and community lecture hall. The project contains subterranean parking for 900 cars. The form for the market-rate high rise towers is developed as a response to site constraints, building setbacks, view shed criteria toward downtown, and shade/shadow considerations at grade. The resultant project is less about defining a prescriptive building solution and more about defining the three-dimensional parameters of the site/societal forces at work which will ultimately lead to architecture.

View from 4th Street bridge

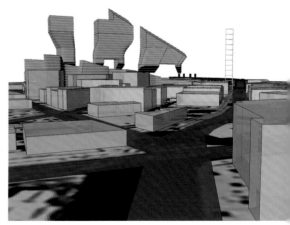

View from 4th Street

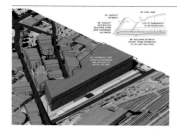

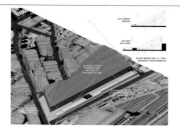

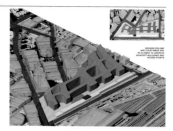

Setbacks, fire lanes, easements of housing building

Sloping height setbacks are applied to housing volume

Housing volume and courtyard are re-aligned to address adjacent buildings and access points

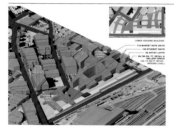

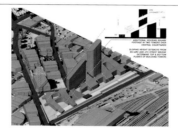

Square footages of housing building

Additional housing area in two towers

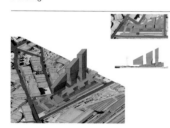

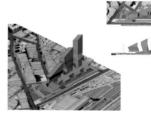

Additional area added at top of towers to increase number of units

Towers are re-positioned to maximize views and natural light

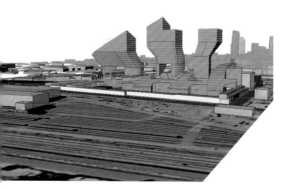

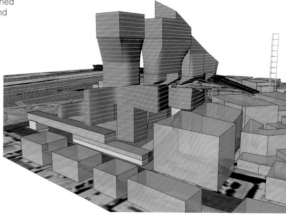

View from East

View from North

Project List

Cobb Residence (1977-1978), Hollywood, California
LaFaille House (1978-1979), Malibu, California
Gibralter Savings and Loan (1979-1980), Los Angeles, California
Five Condominiums (1979-1980), Pasadena, California
Pin Ball House (1980-1984), Los Angeles, California
Chicago Tribune Tower (1980), Chicago, Illinois
Fun House (1980), Los Angeles, California
Adams House (1980-1982), Los Angeles, California
Login House (1980-1982), Malibu, California
Houses X and Y (1981-1982), Malibu, California
Pioneer Commercial Center (1982-1984), Los Angeles, California
Escondido Civic Center (1985), Escondido, California
Lower East Side Housing/Indigent Pavilion (1985), New York, New York
Honey Springs Country Club (1984-1986), San Diego, California
Stacked House (1985), Los Angeles, California
Reservoir House (1985), Los Angeles, California
San Francisco Stadium (1986), San Francisco, California
Yoko Uehara House (1986-1987), Pasadena, California
Tokyo Opera House (1986-1987), Tokyo, California
Multi-Unit Housing (MoCA project) (1988), Los Angeles, California
T&L House (1988), Los Angeles, California
Warner Theater (1990), Culver City, California
A.R.C I T Y (1990-...), Culver City, California
Aronoff Guest House (P&D House) (1991-...), Tarzana, California
Ten Towers (1991-...), Culver City, California
Nara Convention Center (1991), Nara, Japan
MAK (1991), Vienna, Austria
Ibiza Paseo (1992-...), Ibiza, Spain
VLA Sun Drawing Project (1993-...), New Mexico
Santa Monica Science Center (1993-...), Santa Monica, California
Ince Theater (1993-...), Culver City, California
Contemporary Art Center and and Theater (1993), Tours, France
Wagrammerstrasse Housing Project (1994-...), Vienna, Austria
Plaza Vieja (1994-...), Havana, Cuba
Vesey Street Theatre (1994-...), Battery Park City, New York
Children's Museum (1995), Los Angeles, California
LA City Bridge (1995-...), Los Angeles, California
Gasometer D-1 (1995-1996), Vienna, Austria
Samitaur Complex, Phase Two (1991-...)
Samitaur Complex, Phase Three: high-rise towers 3a/3b (1997-...)
Wedgewood Holly Housing-Retail-Office (1998-...), Culver City, California
Louise's: proposed interior of The Box (1996-...), San Francisco, California
Rodeo Dr.-La Cienega: original site plan (1995), Los Angeles, California
Ottakringer Brewery (1996-...), Vienna, Austria
Ibiza Masterplan (1996-...), Ibiza, Spain
CGS (1996), West Los Angeles, California

Jewish Museum San Francisco (1997), San Francisco, California
Monaco Convention Center (1997-...), Port of Monaco, Monaco
White House study (1997), Washington, DC
The Bridge (1998-...), Los Angeles, California
Dusseldorf Harbor (1998-...), Dusseldorf, Germany
What Wall?, including MAK print (1998)
Mills House (1998-...), Hollywood, California
Stanford Learning Center (1998-...), Palo Alto, California
Aronoff Estate (1999-...), Calabassas, California
The Spa (1999-...), Culver City, California
Auschwitz Memorial and Museum (1999-...), Germany
Clerkenwell mixed-use (2000-...), London, England
Oslo Opera House (2000-...), Oslo, Norway
Gateway Office Building (2000-...), Culver City, California
Superblock (2000-...), Culver City, California
Bike Path (2000-...), Culver City and Los Angeles, California
Sagaponac House (2000-...), Long Island, New York
Stora Teatern—New Media and Performance Center (2001-...), Göteborg, Sweden
Supper Club (2001-...), Culver City, California
Caterpillar (2001), Installation at Los Angeles County Museum of Art
Queens Museum of Art (2001-2005), Queens, New York
Wedgewood Holly Complex, (Phase 2, 1998-...)
Mariinsky and New Holland Cultural Center (2001-2003), St. Petersburg, Russia
World Trade Center Exhibition (2001), Max Protech Gallery, New York, New York
Grand Egyptian Museum Competition (2002), Giza, Egypt
Montreal Cultural and Administrative Complex Competition (2002), Montreal, Quebec
San Jose State University School of Art & Design Competition (2002), San Jose, California
Jose Vasconcelos Library of Mexico International Competition (2003), Mexico City, Mexico
Freight Depot (2003-...), Los Angeles, California
New Guangdong Museum Invitational International Competition (2004), Guangzhou, China
Franklin Towers (2004), Hollywood, California
Smithsonian Institute Patent Office Building International Competition (2004), Washington D.C.
Robbins School Competition (2005), Trenton, New Jersey
Guadalajara Library Competition (2005), Guadalajara, Mexico
Gateway (2003-...), Culver City, California
Conjunctive Points Theater Complex (2005-...), Culver City, California
East Los Angeles Housing-Master Plan (2005-...), Los Angeles, California
Sunset Blvd. Housing (2005-...), West Hollywood, California
3555 Hayden (2005-...), Culver City, California
Three Theaters (2005-...), Culver City, California

Realized Works

Triplex Apartments (1974-1976), Playa del Rey, California
Morgenstern Warehouse (1977-1979), Los Angeles, California
708 House (1979-1982), Los Angeles, California
Petal House (1982-1984), Los Angeles, California
World Savings and Loan (1983-1985), Los Angeles, California
Central Housing Office (UCI) (1986-1989), Irvine, California
Lindblade Tower (1987-1989), Culver City, California
Lindblade Tower (1987-1989), Culver City, California
Paramount Laundry (1987-1989), Culver City, California
8522 National Boulevard (1986-1990), Culver City, California
8522 National Boulevard, Conference Room (1986-1990)
8522 National Boulevard, QRC (1988-1990)
8522 National Boulevard, Goalen Group (1988-1990)
8522 National Boulevard, Hybrid Arts (1988-1990)
8522 National Boulevard, SMA (1988-1990)
Gary Group (1988-1990), Culver City, California
The Box (1990-1994), Culver City, California
Lawson Westen House (1993-...), West Los Angeles, California
IRS (1993-1994), Culver City, California
8520 National Annex (1994-2001), Culver City, California
Pittard Sullivan (1994-1997), Culver City, California

Pittard Sullivan, roof addition project (1998)
Samitaur Complex, Phase One (1989-1996), Los Angeles, California
Samitaur Complex, Building C interior (Cobalt Moon) (1997-1999)
Dancing Bleachers (1998), Columbus, Ohio
What Wall? (1998), Culver City, California
Beehive-Annex Conference Center (1996-2001), Culver City, California
Costco (1996), Culver City, California
Wedgewood Holly Complex, Stealth (1993-2001), Culver City, California
Wedgewood Holly Complex, Buildings 1 and 2 (1998-1999)
Wedgewood Holly Complex, Green Umbrella-T minus 30 (1996-1999)
Wedgewood Holly Complex, Pterodactyl (Phase1, 1998-2001)

Bibliography

A. Betsky, "Urbane Renewal", in *Architectural Record*, July 1994, pp. 62-69.

J. Morris Dixon, "The Santa Monica School. What's Its Lasting Contribution?", in *Progressive Architecture*, 76, May 1995, pp. 63-70, 112-114.

J. Dreyfuss, "An Unlikely Dash of Exuberance", in *Los Angeles Times*, 22 October 1978, part VI.

T. Fisher, "Eric Moss and James Joyce", in *Progressive Architecture*, August 1992, pp. 77, 117.

E. Giorgi, "Il grande caos di Culver City", interview with Eric Owen Moss, in *ALIAS* (supplement to *Il Manifesto*), 12 July 2003, pp. 3-4.

J. Giovannini, "Constant Change", in *Architecture*, November 2001, pp. 99-107.

J. Giovannini, "Eric in Wonderland", in *Architecture*, March 2001, pp. 104-112.

J. Giovannini, "L.A. Trouvée", in *Zodiac*, 11, 1994, pp. 70-95.

M. Gottlieb, "Instigating Revolution. School Seeks to Influence the Future Development of Its City", in *California Real Estate Journal*, March 18, 2003, p. 3.

L. Molinari, "Eric Owen Moss e Culver City", in *Lotus*, 109, 2001.

Eric Owen Moss. Architectural monographs, n. 29, Academy Editions, London 1993.

Eric Owen Moss. Buildings and Projects, Rizzoli, New York 1991.

Eric Owen Moss. Buildings and Projects 2, Rizzoli, New York 1995.

Eric Owen Moss. Buildings and Projects 3, Rizzoli, New York 2002.

E.O. Moss, *Gnostic Architecture*, Monacelli, New York 1999.

E.O. Moss, "Out of Place is the One Right Place", in P. Noever (ed.), *The End of Architecture? Documents and Manifestos*, Prestel-Verlag, Monaco 1993, pp. 60-71.

E.O. Moss, "What's New?", in *The Berlage Institute Report* (Hunch: *109 Provisional Attempts to Address Six Simple and Hard Questions About What Architects Do Today and Where Their Profession Might Go Tomorrow*), 6/7, 2003, pp. 338-339.

N. Ouroussoff, "Manipulating the Myths of Suburbia", in *Los Angeles Times*, *Calendar* section, 3 March 2002, pp. 63, 83.

N. Ouroussoff, "The Latest Alteration of a City's Industrial Fabric", in *Los Angeles Times*, 26 October 1996, pp. F1, F10.

J. Ringen, "Culver City Renaissance", in *Metropolis*, January 2002, pp. 68-72.

P. Scott Cohen, B. Hodge (editor), *Eric Owen Moss. The Box*, Princeton Architectural Press, New York 1996.

M. Speaks, "Due architetture recenti. Culver City, California", in *Domus*, 826, May 2000, pp. 42-53.

J. Steele, *Lawson-Westen House (Architecture in Detail)*, Phaidon Press, London 1995.

A. Vidler, *Warped Space. Art, Architecture, and Anxiety in Modern Culture*, The MIT Press, Cambridge 2000.

L. Whiteson, "Packing Up and Heading West", in *Los Angeles Times*, 29 January 1996, pp. E1, E4.

Biography

Eric Owen Moss, Principal and Lead Designer
Eric Owen Moss Architects, Culver City, CA

Eric Owen Moss was born and raised in Los Angeles, California. He received a Bachelor of Arts from the University of California at Los Angeles in 1965. Moss continued his education, earning his Masters of Architecture from the University of California at Berkeley, College of Environmental Design in 1968 and a second Masters of Architecture from Harvard University Graduate School of Design in 1972.

Through the years Eric Owen Moss has worked extensively to revitalize a once defunct industrial tract in Culver City, California. The introduction of vibrant designs that challenge the boundaries of technology and foster creativity has successfully created jobs and community morale through the development of the project known as Conjunctive Points. His efforts have gained recognition locally, nationally and internationally. In 2003 Eric Owen Moss was awarded the Business Week/Architectural Record Award for the design and construction of the Stealth. This award applauds uniting excellence in business as well as design. Eric Owen Moss designs have consistently gained recognition for innovative building techniques, community development

and job creation, as well as excellence in design.

Eric Owen Moss received the AIA/LA Medal in 1998 for the achievement of an outstanding body of architectural works. He is a Fellow of the American Institute of Architecture and was a recipient of the Distinguished Alumni Award for the University of California at Berkeley in 2003.

Teaching
Southern California Institute of Architecture: Director
Harvard Graduate School of Design, Cambridge
Yale University, New Haven
University of Applied Arts, Vienna
University of California Los Angeles
Rice University, Houston
Columbia University, New York
DIS Architecture and Design, Copenhagen, Denmark

Selected Awards
Business Week/Architectural Record Awards: Ogilvy and Mather, 2003
World Trade Center Competition for LMDC: Semi-finalist, 2003
The Chicago Athenaeum American Architecture Award: 3505 Hayden Avenue, 2003
AIA/LA Design Award, Interior Architecture: Caterpillar, 2003
33rd Los Angeles Architectural Awards Ogilvy and Mather, 2003
Alumni Association Distinguished Alumnus Award: University

of California, Berkeley, 2003
AIA/LA Design Merit Award: Medschool.com, 2002
NEXT LA Award: Mariinsky Theater, 2002
AIA/CC Design Honor Award: Ogilvy and Mather, 2002
Westside Urban Forum: Ogilvy and Mather, 2002
AIA/LA Gold Medal for Design Achievement, 2001
AIA/LA Design Award: Ogilvy and Mather, 2001
NEXT LA Award: Ten Towers, 2001
Los Angeles Business Council Design Award: Ogilvy and Mather, 2001
Progressive Architecture Design Award: Spa, 2000
Los Angeles Urban Beautification Award: T-30 Films, 2000
Saflex Glass Design Award: T-30 Films, 2000
DuPont Benedictus Award: T-30 Films, 2000
AIA/LA Honor Award for Design: T-30 Films, 1999
Academy Award in Architecture, American Academy of Arts and Letters, New York 1999
NEXT LA Award: Pterodactyl, 1999
AIA/CC Design Award: 3535 Hayden Avenue, 1998
Los Angeles Urban Beautification Award: Cineon Kodak, 1998
NEXT LA Award: Gasometer D-1, 1997
AIA/LA Divine Details Award: Metafor, 1997
AIA/LA Honor Award: Cineon Kodak, 1996
Progressive Architecture Design Award: Ince Theatre, 1995
AIA/CC Design Honor Award: The Box, 1995

DuPont Benedictus Award: The Box, 1995
AIA/LA Design Award: Lawson/Westen House, 1994
AIA/LA Design Award: The Box, 1994
AIA National Interior Design Award of Excellence: Lawson/Westen House, 1994
AIA/LA Design Award: Lawson-Westen House, 1993
AIA National Citation: Excellence in International Architecture Book Publishing, 1992
Progressive Architecture Design Award: Cineon Kodak, 1992
Progressive Architecture Design Award: Aronoff Guest House, 1992
AIA National Interior Design Award of Excellence: Gary Group, 1992
AIA National Interior Design Award of Excellence: 8522 National Boulevard, 1992
AIA/CC Urban Design/Adaptive Re-Use Award: 8522 National Boulevard, 1991
AIA National Honor Award: Central Housing Office, University of California, Irvine, 1989
AIA National Honor Award: 8522 National Boulevard, 1988

Selected Winning Competitions
New Holland Cultural Center: 1st Place, St. Petersburg, Russia, 2003
Mariinsky Theater: 1st Place, St. Petersburg, Russia, 2003
Queens Museum of Art: 1st Place, Queens, New York, 2001

Stanford University
Learning Lab: 1st Place,
Palo Alto, California, 1998
Jewish Museum San
Francisco: 1st Place, San
Francisco, California, 1997
Jose Vasconcelos Library
of Mexico: 2nd Place,
Mexico City, Mexico, 2003

Selected Recent
Exhibitions
La Biennale di Venezia,
"Metamorph", Giardini
Arsenale: Venice, Italy,
2004
"Finalist Schemes for
the Biblioteca de Mexico",
Biblioteca de Mexico,
Mexico City, Mexico, 2004
"US Design 1975-2000":
Denver Art Museum,
Denver, Colorado; Bass
Museum of Art, Miami,
Florida; American Craft
Museum, New York,
New York; Housten Art
Museum, Housten, Texas,
2004
"Sao Paulo Biennale
of Architecture and Design",
Sao Paulo, Brazil, 2004
"Architectures
Experimentales",
Collection du Frac Center,
Orleans, France, 2003
"A New World Trade
Center: Design Proposals":
Max Protetch Gallery, New
York, New York
European Tour: Cube
Gallery, Manchester,
England;
Deutsches Achitektur
Museum, Frankfurt,
Germany;
Arkitekturmuseet,
Stockholm, Sweden, 2003
La Biennale di Venezia,
"A New World Trade
Center", American
Pavillion, Venice, Italy,
2002

La Biennale di Venezia,
"New Mariinsky Cultural
Center", Russian Pavillion,
Venice, Italy, 2002
"Architecture for a New
Millennium": MOCA,
Taipei, Taiwan; Top-Center
Cultural Center, Taichung,
Taiwan; Macau Museum
of Art, Macau, China;
Overseas Museum,
Guangzhou, China; MOCA,
Beijing, China, 2003
"What's Shakin'? New
Architecture in LA",
MOCA, Los Angeles,
California, 2002
"Designing the Future: The
Queens Museum of Art
& The New York City
Building", Queens
Museum of Art, Queens,
New York, 2002
La Biennale di Venezia,
American Pavilion, Venice,
Italy, 1996

Project Credits

"They were born never
to live in peace and quiet
themselves, and to prevent
the rest of the world from
doing so."
Thucydides

George Elian
Dennis Ige
Nick Seirup
Jay Vanos
Scott Nakao
Greg Baker
Janek Tabencki Dombrowa
Paul Groh
John Bencher
Dolan Daggett
Eric McNevin

Photo Credits

Tom Bonner 36, 57, 59, 61,
77, 78, 79, 82, 83, 96, 97,
100-101, 103, 104, 105 right,
109, 110-111, 112, 113,
115, 118, 121 bottom, 123,
125, 126, 127, 218, 219,
220, 221, 222 top
Todd Conversano 63, 215
top
Micah Heimlich 65, 67, 68,
69, 99, 121 top, 128, 129
Paul Groh 71, 72, 84, 93,
95, 102, 105 bottom left,
116-117, 134 bottom left,
135, 177, 225, 226-227
Raul Garcia 86, 87 bottom
right, 88, 89, 144 top, 230
right
Don Dimster 120
Grace Pae 132, 134 right
and bottom right
Tom Raymont 137, 144
bottom
Douglas Hill 210, 211
bottom
Doug Parker 211 top
Tim Street-Porter 212, 213
Alex Vertikoff 214, 216, 217
Scott Smith 215 bottom
Peter Cook 222 bottom
Frank Jackson 223 top
Grant Mudford 223 bottom
left
Donatella Brun 223 bottom
right